# The Language of the Soul

# Also by Mark Nepo

**NONFICTION**

*The Fifth Season*

*You Don't Have to Do It Alone*

*Falling Down and Getting Up*

*Surviving Storms*

*The Book of Soul*

*Drinking from the River of Light*

*More Together Than Alone*

*Things That Join the Sea and the Sky*

*The One Life We're Given*

*The Endless Practice*

*Seven Thousand Ways to Listen*

*Finding Inner Courage*

*Unlearning Back to God*

*The Exquisite Risk*

*The Book of Awakening*

**FICTION**

*As Far as the Heart Can See*

**POETRY**

*The Half-Life of Angels*

*The Way Under the Way*

*Inside the Miracle*

*Reduced to Joy*

*Surviving Has Made Me Crazy*

*Suite for the Living*

Praise for *The Language of the Soul*

"Mark Nepo has soul-stirring language coursing through his veins. In *The Language of the Soul*, Mark has gathered some of the most potent words alive in our world today and held them up to the light to reveal their full depth and beauty. This book is a stunning pilgrimage to the heart of language. You will never look at words in the same way again."
—Beth Kempton, bestselling author of *Wabi Sabi*

"*The Language of the Soul* invites readers to consider the evocative, fluid nature of words. On every page, Mark Nepo offers insights that awaken the heart and stir the mind. This is not just a book to read, but to revisit time and again, an essential guide for anyone longing to live with more authenticity and depth."
—April Dávila, award-winning author and writing coach

"In this fascinating lexicon of soul-powered language, Nepo demonstrates the power of particular words to expand the spirit, revivify the heart, and point you toward your original nature. Original, inspirational, and deeply instructive, this book opens your ear to the voice of God and helps you remember how sacredness sounds."
—Mark Matousek, author of *Emerson, The Stoics, and Me: Timeless Wisdom for Living an Authentic Life*

“Throughout this heart-opening journey, Mark Nepo tenderly guides us to uncover the language of our soul, the root that attaches our lives to the greater, foundational life of Spirit. In doing so, Mark invites us to join him in discovering the ground of meaning and the life-force that helps us embody a deeper, more authentic way of being. This is a must-read for anyone seeking to live from the consciousness of their core.”

—Karin A. Nobile, program director,
Mercy by the Sea Retreat and Conference Center

*Inhabiting Wonder*

*Acre of Light*

*Fire Without Witness*

*God, the Maker of the Bed, and the Painter*

**EDITOR**

*Deepening the American Dream*

**RECORDINGS**

*The Fifth Season*

*You Don't Have to Do It Alone*

*Falling Down and Getting Up*

*Surviving Storms*

*The Book of Soul*

*Flames That Light the Heart* (video course)

*More Together Than Alone*

*The One Life We're Given*

*Inside the Miracle* (expanded, 2015)

*Reduced to Joy*

*The Endless Practice*

*Seven Thousand Ways to Listen*

*Staying Awake*

*Holding Nothing Back*

*As Far As the Heart Can See*

*The Book of Awakening*

*Finding Inner Courage*

*Finding Our Way in the World*

*Inside the Miracle* (1996)

# The Language of the Soul

*How the Words You Choose Shape the Life You Live*

Mark Nepo

ST. MARTIN'S ESSENTIALS
NEW YORK

The information in this book is not intended to replace the advice of the reader's own physician or other medical professional. You should consult a medical professional in matters relating to health, especially if you have existing medical conditions, and before starting, stopping, or changing the dose of any medication you are taking. Individual readers are solely responsible for their own health-care decisions. The author and the publisher do not accept responsibility for any adverse effects individuals may claim to experience, whether directly or indirectly, from the information contained in this book.

First published in the United States by St. Martin's Essentials,
an imprint of St. Martin's Publishing Group

*EU Representative:* Macmillan Publishers Ireland Ltd, 1st Floor, The Liffey Trust Centre,
117–126 Sheriff Street Upper, Dublin 1, D01 YC43



www.stmartins.com

Library of Congress Cataloging-in-Publication Data

Names: Nepo, Mark author
Title: The language of the soul : how the words you choose shape the life
you live / Mark Nepo.
Description: First edition. | New York : St. Martin's Essentials, 2026.
Includes bibliographical references.
Identifiers: LCCN 2025053144 | ISBN 9781250404237 trade paperback |
ISBN 9781250404244 ebook
Subjects: LCSH: Meditations | Spiritual life | Communication—Religious
aspects
Classification: LCC BL624.2 .N47225 2026
LC record available at https://lccn.loc.gov/2025053144



First Edition: 2026

10 9 8 7 6 5 4 3 2 1

*For anyone trying to make sense of being here*

*My words are only fingers pointing at the moon.*
*Make sure you look at the moon!*

—Attributed to Buddha

# Contents

# The Language of the Soul

# The Life of Words

For more than half a century, I've been a poet, a seeker, a student of wonder, and a witness of suffering, committed to discovering and practicing the art of being human. Over the years, I've lost and found my way countless times. Like a prospector, I've sifted through the dirt on path after path, surprised to find gold in a word here and a word there that might help us live. This book gathers the nuggets of meaning found along the way.

Toward that end, I've gone through all my books, collecting the words and phrases that, when held to the light, reveal gateways of transformation. And each word or phrase, when traced back, can illuminate the Web of Kinship we need to inhabit to be as alive as possible. The origin of each word or phrase, if related to, can help us stay alive and connected.

I confess that I've always been fascinated with the origin of words, not because I'm a word geek. But because I've found, time and again, that the original forms of words, in all cultures, are more whole, more faceted, more substantial, and, ultimately, more useful. In the same way that mountains, rivers, and forests erode over time, words erode. They break apart, split, fragment, and lose their original reach and impact. And so, I became a seeker of origins.

Since the beginning of time, we all keep reaching for the one language that binds us. One example dates back to the 1800s, where an amalgamated, pidgin form of expression called wantok developed in the South Pacific. It was spoken by lonely sailors who, when docking in New Guinea, were hoping to meet someone who might speak their native tongue. They were desperate to speak directly with another, with no intermediary or translator. They wanted only the wantok or *one-talk* under all their dialects and inflections. Isn't this what we all want? Isn't this what we hope each day will bring?

I have chosen these words in an effort to illuminate as many foundational expressions as I could find across time and many cultures. And each of these 228 words, phrases, and mythic notions—gathered from thirty-one languages and traditions—affirms our journey of being a Spirit in a body in time on Earth. I hope one or more of these deep expressions will bring you into the timeless field of knowing where we can learn together. I hope one or more of these words will serve as a comfort and source of strength, and offer you a sense of home in the days ahead.

# A Guide to This Journey

Let me offer a few thoughts about the structure of this book. My intent is to have this endeavor be more than a glossary or a dictionary but rather a hands-on, heart-opening journey that can be helpful to your life—more like a toolbox or first-aid kit that has gathered pathways and instruments from many traditions across the ages.

In an attempt to make this as accessible and relatable as possible, the chapters are thematic, each exploring an archetypal passage, each focusing on how we might live more completely and more fully in relation to life and each other. Each chapter contains word clusters that deepen our understanding of words and their origins as they explore that chapter's theme. And each word cluster is followed by a question to walk with, as a way to bring whatever moves you back into your daily life.

What holds these word clusters together is a book-length conversation, which takes the form of an ongoing commentary that frames the word clusters with reflections and questions. This conversation over time offers historical, mythic, and personal stories that demonstrate the power of language to initiate our journey of Spirit and to restore us to our basic human nature.

As you make your way through the book, I encourage you to relate to the original meanings of these words and phrases. They are more than just concepts or curious histories. Each is alive and dynamic. Each points to a current in living that we have to navigate and, when personalized, each word or phrase invites a practice that can return us to what matters.

So, I urge you to read this book slowly, over months, like a diver who combs the ocean floor, not sure for what; a diver who comes up to live their life, who lets the deep inform their life, who returns to dive again, and again. For this book is meant to be a companion on the journey.

I also urge you to keep a journal in which you can relate to the words and phrases that speak to you. To personalize the meanings as you go, I suggest that you pause when a word and what it points to moves you. In your journal:

- Try to name what aspect of living the word is referring to.
- Then, describe how that dynamic appears in your life.
- Finally, identify one small and specific way you can work to better meet this dynamic.

For example, if we're looking at the word *riptide*, we can see that it refers to "any strong crosscurrent that could be dangerous to a swimmer." We all face such crosscurrents within us and between us. So, you could explore this word in your journal this way:

- Explore how the notion of a riptide might appear as the crosscurrent of caring for a family member we still love who is harsh and even cruel.
- In your own life, describe such a loved one and explore how you might better meet this dynamic of giving care without exposing yourself to harm.
- Then, identify one small and specific way you can begin to navigate this crosscurrent.

My hope is that all the structures, stories, and questions woven in these pages will make this less a reference book and more a journey of inference; more a web of connections that will help you know your place in the world, while discovering how the world can healthfully insinuate its depth and breadth in you.

# Words Are Thresholds

Though this book is organized thematically, all the words are listed here for easy access in your day-to-day journey.

The 228 words explored are from these thirty-one languages and traditions: Akan, Arabic, Blackfoot, Buddhist, Chinese, Danish, English, German, Greek, Hawaiian, Hebrew, Hindi, Iroquois, Japanese, Latin, Lebanese, Mexican, various Native American words, Norse, Polish, Portuguese, Rwandan, Sanskrit, Senegalese, Spanish, Sufi, Swahili, Tibetan, Yiddish, Yoruba, and Zulu.

fellow: 130
foreign: 130
forgive: 261
friendship: 130
gacaca: 134
Ganesh: 233
generosity: 108
genius: 26
ginosko: 266
grace: 108
Great Spoked Wheel: 137
guru: 90
hachnasat orchim: 147
haecceitas: 85
haggadah: 237
hanamuke: 66
Hinayana: 27
hineni: 69
holm: 111
honor: 266
hsien: 55
human: 138
humility: 28
hygge: 245
ichor: 163
idiot: 209
ikigai: 163
'ilm: 97

# A Place to Begin

*In Africa, there's a small bird known as the greater honey guide. It has a black throat, a yellow shoulder, and bold white streaks in its tail. Throughout time, the honey guide has led tribal members to beehives where they can retrieve the native honey.*

*In their original state, words are such guides to the honey hidden in life. When drawn to a word, we must open our heart and follow the word to the honey it will lead us to. I encourage you to track the honey guides in this book that touch you and speak to you. Spend time with them. Find your greater honey guides, here and in the world, and let them be your teachers. Ask them to lead you to the sweetness waiting inside every moment.*

*And so, this gathering of words is an invitation to experience the Oneness that all words point to. I encourage you to not just examine these words but to relate to them and all they point to, so you might feel the magic they indicate and represent. For each word has been carried in the river of time, and when we hear them and speak them, we drink from that river.*

*Paradoxically, language is the irrepressible conveyor of all that can't be said. Somehow, our effort to utter and preserve what we experience leaves a scattering of jewels that we call words, which reflect the intangible elements of life.*

*I welcome you, then, into a lifelong conversation with the oldest and most reliable of words and what they open. For language is the tether between worlds. In truth, as Buddha suggests, every word is a finger pointing at the moon. Every word is a placeholder. Every word is a marker left on the trail of life. At their best, words lead us into the currents of life that always live below the names we give them.*

*Yet, in time, we often mistake the word for what it represents or points to. In time, we stop at the silhouette of the word* tree *and forget that it points to this majestic, wooden thing that grows out of the ground. In time, we stop at the silhouette of the word* star *and forget that it points to a mass of light larger than the planet we live on. In time, we stop at the silhouette of the word* God *and forget that it points to the Totality of the Living Universe that carries us all.*

*At their deepest and freshest, words have an awakening power, if we can enter the realms they point to rather than collect them as labels. In their original stature, words are doorways. And so, in unfolding these numinous words and phrases, I urge you to walk through them and to relate to the expanse and depth they reveal.*

# The Nature of the Soul

*Almost forty years ago, I was being wheeled into surgery to have a cancerous rib removed from my back. Suddenly, as I saw the fluorescent lights flip by above me, as I heard the squeak of the metal wheels whisking me to the operating room, I slipped below all names. Like a dolphin slipping below the noisy slap of waves, I was, for the moment, in the everlasting world of Depth and Spirit. Everything moved slower below the surface without a name. And it was clear to me that this nameless depth baptizes us in the raw essence of things with the elemental shimmer of life that animates and connects us, again and again.*

*That moment changed my life. While I am still the person Mark, who turns when you call my name, I know that the essence of who I am and what I am arises from that nameless depth that lives below all names. This deepened my call as a poet and changed my relationship to words. For words are only markers for what can't be named. Words only point the way. What matters is the Depth of Spirit that enlivens all things before they are named. The task of the poet is to invoke that Depth of Spirit to show itself, however briefly, through the images and stories we can conjure through the brushwork of our truth and tenderness. And so, any word that is worthy helps us live—but only when we open it and drink there.*

*This chapter explores the nature of the soul as a conduit between the inner life and the outer life and how closely the heart serves as an instrument of the soul: helping us retrieve the nameless resources that enliven us and carry us, and how the heart, then, helps us to navigate the world with our full being and aliveness.*

## A WORD CLUSTER

become
blessing

When God is asked in the Torah for His name, a reply comes from the unseeable, "I am Becoming . . ." At once, *Becoming* emanates two meanings. As a noun, it suggests that God is a process, that the sacred reveals itself in a life of transformation and unfolding. As a verb, it suggests that God is still emerging, still not completely defined, beautifully as unfinished as we are.

By saying His name is "I am Becoming," God is showing us how to live fully in the world—as unfinished and emergent. You could say that the aim of any sacred becoming is not to arrive at any finished state, but to taste everything in our brush with life and thereby know, through experience, the hint of what is holy.

The kind of courage this requires is both real and noble. Real in the fact that the only way to *become* is through facing our experience directly and committing to our continual emergence. And noble in how we stay faithful to what's possible if we keep sparking tomorrow with who we are today. The mystical Persian poet of the thirteenth century Attar, who was an immediate ancestor to Rumi, affirms this kind of courage when he says, "For your Soul, seek Spiritual knowledge from what is Real."

How, then, do we find the courage to stay in process and to keep emerging? How do we encourage the heart to blossom? How do we go about trying to embody wisdom? Through a sacred becoming.

If we don't engage in life and participate, we don't manifest our being in the world. We don't become. The German philosopher Immanuel Kant spoke of such becoming as *self-positing*, and his contemporary Friedrich Hegel spoke of such becoming as *self-owning*.

To manifest our soul in the world by inhabiting our life fully raises a corollary to Hamlet's famous soliloquy. Alongside *to be or not to be*, we're called *to become or not to become*. For, if it's worth being here, then it's imperative that we hold nothing back and give our all to the days as they unfold.

The word *become* traces back to the Old English *becuman*,

which means "come to a place." And the place we come to, if authentic and kind, is the place of blessing. In Tony Kushner's epic play *Angels in America*, a deep refrain occurs when the main character, Prior, says repeatedly with increasing urgency and conviction that he wants more life. In his notes, Kushner reveals that what stirred this motif was his discovery that the Hebrew word for *blessing* means "more life." This is the blessing that comes from being educated by the heart—we are given more life. This is the blessing I wish for everyone—that as a fish grows stronger for having healthy and muscular gills, you are given more life for having an expansive and well-tuned heart.

### A *Question to Walk With*

In your journal, describe one way you're still becoming, and one way you are still unfinished. Later, in conversation with a friend or loved one, discuss how your process of becoming is giving you more life.

### Our Conversation Over Time

*The essence of our living can only be pointed to, never contained. This is the true province of words: to point to and open, not to label and contain.*

*Imagine Buddha in his moment of enlightenment, of being lighted from within. I doubt if he knew he was aglow. In fact, when Buddha rose from under the Bodhi tree, it is said a monk approached him in utter amazement at his luminosity and asked, "O Holy One, what are you? You must be a god."*

*Buddha, not thinking of himself as anything but present, answered, "No . . . not a god," and kept walking. But the dazzled monk persisted, "Then you must be a deva," and Buddha stopped and said, "No . . . not a deva," and kept walking. Still, the monk pursued him, saying, "Then you must be Brahma himself!"*

*At this, Buddha simply uttered, "No." The monk, confused, implored, "Then what are you? Tell me, please—what are you?!" Buddha could not repress his joy and sighed, "I am awake."*

*Can it be that our purpose, no matter where we go, no matter what we're told, is simply to be awake? Can it be that when awake, language keeps us true and when asleep or numb, language covers us up?*

## A WORD CLUSTER

bodhisatta
bodhisattva

Buddha is often referred to as the *bodhisatta*, which means "one on the path to awakening." This differs from the term *bodhisattva*, which means "one who has awakened, but who has chosen to stay in earthly relationship with others in support of a mutual enlightenment." A bodhisattva chooses to stay in the tangle of human existence and suffering rather than leave the earthly plane, because without the love of others, heaven is a vacant palace.

This raises the twin call for every soul: to pursue our own awakening and to keep others company on their journey of awakening. Some traditions insist that the journey of awakening is an individual path, while others insist that the journey of awakening arises from relationship and community. In actuality, the singular and communal paths to awakening inform each other.

In Theravada Buddhism, a bodhisattva is considered rare. Yet I believe we each have the capacity to be a bodhisattva, if we love each other into the truth of our being. Just as we carry *X* and *Y* chromosomes, every soul has the inherent capacity to actualize its love in the world as a bodhisattva.

In Mahayana Buddhism, a bodhisattva is considered a spiritually devoted person committed to manifesting heaven on earth. In this tradition, we are all spiritually capable of facing the truth of our days with nothing between our soul and life. In this way, the fullness of our soul is not rare but simply dormant, like seeds that wait to be watered.

Where are you, then, in the path of your individual awakening? And where are you in the work of keeping others company on the path of their awakening? How are these twin paths shaping you?

## *A Question to Walk With*

In your journal, describe the next step in your awakening that is completely yours, which no one can do for you. What is keeping you from taking this step? Later, in conversation with a friend or loved one, describe how your individual journeys affect each other. Explore how your paths in being authentic are entwined.

## Our Conversation Over Time

*Of all the places it can nest, it's fascinating how a bluebird will fly through a small hole into a small box posted in the middle of an open yard or field. Clearly, the small pocket of air in the bluebird house is comprised of the same air that makes up the entire sky. Yet the bluebird makes its nest and then flies from the little air into the big air and back. This is the pattern of its life.*

*This is a great metaphor for the nature of the soul and how it lives in relationship to the uncontainable life of Spirit that is everywhere. For the bird of our soul flies from the nest of our little life into the big, uncontainable life and back, day after day. As I suggested above, the purpose of the soul is to be a living conduit between our little life and the big life we are a part of, between our individual time and the expanse of all time, between the gestures of love and truth and the galaxy of love and truth.*

*In many ways, the original and ancient meanings of words are like bluebird houses that hold a small portion of Eternity in which we can build our nest.*

## A WORD CLUSTER

brilliance
El
Al

We think of the physicist Albert Einstein as conceptually brilliant, and the dancer Mikhail Baryshnikov as breathtakingly brilliant, and the Impressionist Claude Monet as creatively brilliant. But before the modern mind defined *brilliance* as "the singular appearance of uncanny skill," the word meant an emanation of being that was brilliant like the sun. Before brilliance described an unprecedented moment of achievement, the word referred to "the intense brightness of light" coming forth from a source. The original notion of brilliance describes an ultimate manifestation of being.

In this regard, Einstein, Baryshnikov, and Monet may have been exceptional in what they accomplished, but this was because each was brilliant in the emanation of their being, brilliant in *how* they thought, danced, and painted.

This emanation of life-force is at the heart of all the spiritual traditions. If we trace how the major traditions of the Middle East unfolded, we find that Judaism, Christianity, and Islam stem from the same Source, and probably the same language. All originally called God either *El* or *Al*, which means "The One" or "That One which expresses itself uniquely through all beings." From this arose the sacred names Elohim (Hebrew) and Allah (Arabic). Imagine, we are all expressions of the same Original Being, and much of our lives are spent recovering that deep knowing.

And so, our individual brilliance, or emanation of light, replicates the emanation of Spirit which expresses itself uniquely through all beings. Our individual light is a small, enduring fractal of the Universal Light. Our brilliance, when not muffled or denied, connects us to the Original Being at the heart of all spiritual paths.

In truth, to devote ourselves to the modern sense of brilliance keeps us striving for individual greatness, while to devote ourselves to the original sense of brilliance lets us experience the greatness of life.

## *A Question to Walk With*

In your journal, describe your sense of a brilliant achievement that you're working toward. What is the reward and cost for you as you work toward this? Later, in conversation with a friend or loved one, describe someone who emanates light and warmth in the original sense of brilliance. Where do these qualities live in you?

## Our Conversation Over Time

*I was having lunch with Olasope Oyelaran, a linguist from Nigeria. As we talked, he brought languages alive, describing them like tropical plants. He spoke of them as rooted things that sprout and reach in all directions for the light. He marveled that there are seven thousand living languages on Earth. And these are only the ones we know of. The music of his African voice flowed beneath his overtones of English. Listening to him affirmed the things that come before us and which, thankfully, outlast us.*

*That night, as I settled under the covers, with the lights out, I heard our yellow Lab breathe as the wind announced the stars. There, in the silence that's never quite silent, I realized that, if there are at least seven thousand ways to speak, there are at least seven thousand ways to listen. And just how few we know.*

*The many ways to listen have been reaching into me for years. To enter deep listening, I've had to learn how to keep emptying and opening, how to keep beginning. I've had to lean in to all I don't understand, accepting that I am changed by what I hear.*

## A WORD CLUSTER

### genius

Like the word *brilliance*, we have elevated the word *genius* to signify some extraordinary capacity or skill. But the word genius originally meant "attendant spirit." Everyone has an attendant spirit, or inner voice, or guardian angel. This is where the word *genie* comes from. And so, the archetype of Aladdin's lamp is not rubbing a lamp to get what you want, but embracing your life until your attendant spirit shows up to guide you. This gives added meaning to William Blake's proverb "Straight is the road to improvement, but crooked is the road to genius." How, then, can you call on and relate to your attendant spirit?

One clue comes from the deep insight of William Butler Yeats when he said, "Genius is a crisis that joins the buried self to the daily mind for brief moments." We all have access to our attendant spirit when we embrace our life and face what is ours to face. When loving and truthful, our attendant spirit shows up.

## *A Question to Walk With*

In your journal, explore a few specific ways you can be more loving and truthful, and how this might bring you closer to your attendant spirit.

## A WORD CLUSTER

Hinayana
Mahayana

Once we commit to a life of becoming, once we seek the blessing of more life, once we release a deeper form of brilliance, once we stay in conversation with our attendant spirit, we are returned to the perennial question: Do we go it alone or make our way together?

These choices are represented by the two prominent Buddhist traditions: Hinayana Buddhism, which seeks personal enlightenment (*Hinayana* means "little raft"), and Mahayana Buddhism, which seeks a mutual enlightenment with others (*Mahayana* means "big raft").

To make it through this life, we need a raft. Whether that raft is small or has room for many, having something sturdy to carry us is essential. When life becomes difficult, we either retreat into solitude or extend ourselves further into relationship. When fearful and in pain, do we push others off our raft or bring them onboard? The type of world we live in depends on how we respond to this question, again and again.

## *A Question to Walk With*

In your journal, describe the raft that carries you through life. Is it small or big? Are you satisfied with your raft as it is? How might you amend or repair the raft that carries you through life? Who taught you about the kind of raft you should have?

## A WORD CLUSTER

humility
intellectual
iwa

There are three ways to inhabit integrity: through the grounded gesture of humility, through the combined openness of heart and mind, and through the joined moment when being and doing are the same.

The word *humility* traces back to the word *humus*, which means "soil or earth." Inevitably, the act of humility grounds us by bringing us back to earth. One of the inadvertent rewards for falling down is that our insistence on where we're going is interrupted. We're forced to return to a greater perspective. Being humbled—broken of our pride and intent—opens us to life other than our own. From here, we can begin again.

If we look back far enough in the Western tradition, we can see that the word *intellectual* originally meant both heart and mind, but as we moved through the Industrial Age, the use of the heart was cleaved from the use of the mind. Somehow, our preoccupation with everything mechanical divorced us from the Whole. And the integrated seat of contemplation that is honored in most cultures was somehow muted and lost in the Western world. As the rational mind became dominant, the workings of the heart ceased to be intuitive but were considered irrational, and empiricists and romantics were pitted against each other, until those sharp with reasoning are now called cynical and those replete with feeling are now called sentimental.

Yet, like humility, it's the unified embrace of our heart and mind that grounds us in a larger perspective. It's the openness of heart and mind that lets us rejoin with other life.

Despite our want to break things down, the Unity of Life

remains the foundation of all relationship. In the Yoruba language, spoken in West Africa, there is one word for being and doing, *iwa* (ee-wah). The word means "all that informs your existence." Beauty is part of your iwa, and relationship and community are part of your iwa. If I were to say, "I know your iwa," it means I know your history, your dreams, your strengths, and your frailties. It means I know what waits under your words and between your hesitations. It means I know the unity of your life. Iwa refers to an all-embracing way of relationship. Iwa evokes a quality of care that connects us to everything.

Isn't this the aim of all relationship: to know each other intimately and comprehensively, to know each other's history and dreams, to know each other's strengths and frailties? And given how we're tossed about so harshly by the storms of experience, our challenge is to see our way through, so we can know the unity of our own life, of those we love, and of life itself. It remains a mythic passage: that no matter the size of the storm, our work is to stay in relationship to the stream of life, the way a tired fish thrown from a waterfall relies on the current to receive it and carry it along.

## *A Question to Walk With*

In your journal, describe a moment of humility in which you were grounded and returned to a larger perspective. Then, describe a moment of unified perception in which your heart and mind were knit together. What did these moments open for you? Later, in conversation with a friend or loved one, say to each other, "I know your iwa." Then, bear witness to how you know each other's history, dreams, strengths, and frailties.

## Our Conversation Over Time

*In 1836, Ralph Waldo Emerson published his seminal essay "Nature" in which he declared that the divine and immanent energy of Spirit is everywhere, that nature itself is a living expression of the irrepressible give and take of life's energy. This belief in the natural world as a conduit for the spiritual world became the foundation of transcendentalism. Essential to Emerson's worldview is the role of experience as our constant teacher. This coincides with the Native American and Hindu traditions, which reinforce that everything and everyone is a teacher, if we can stay present and in conversation with life through its particulars.*

*One of Emerson's profound insights is revealed in his quote:*

> Every [person's] condition is a solution in hieroglyphic to those inquiries [we] would put. [We] act it as life, before [we] apprehend it as truth.

*We each have our own language of wisdom and each experience adds a word to that language which we must decipher. In this way, accepting experience as our teacher lets us uncover the language of our soul. And so, there's no foreknowledge outside of experience. Insight and wisdom are the result of processing our experience, one pain and one joy at a time. As we go, the earned and felt language we arrive at accrues meaning. Within the language of our wisdom, each word is a tool that can help us make our way, the way a carpenter uses his tools to build a bridge.*

## A WORD CLUSTER

kenshō
khanti-parami
lebak
sirr

In Japanese, *kenshō* means "seeing into one's nature." By staying open to insight and investing time and care into our wonder, curiosity, creativity, and compassion, we deepen our conversation with our inborn nature. In the Zen tradition, kenshō has come to represent the intuitive way of learning that awakens us en route to beholding and being held by the Buddha nature that resides in each of us.

With regard to the inner journey, kenshō can be understood as the path toward self-realization, or finding our place as a living part in the Living Universe, as a grain of sand refined by Eternity. This sense of largesse relates to the Sanskrit word *sunyata*, which means "emptiness" or the spaciousness that holds us. Sunyata also refers to "the original countenance one had before one was born."

All this implies that we come from some unnamable reservoir of life-force, which is our family of Original Presence, a presence we carry within like a seed of great love waiting to be manifest in the world. This meeting and re-meeting with Original Presence is the inner food that can only be digested through the practice of introspection, reflection, and understanding—which all take time.

There is a long-standing sense in the mystical traditions that our initiation of insight into our true nature is sudden, arriving with the power of lightning, like a moment of revelation through which our sense of the world is changed—all at once.

However, once awakened to our true nature, we're required to enhance and deepen that insight through experience and study, through working with teachers—treating the path of our understanding as a long road we must care for and stay committed to.

This brings us to one of the ten Buddhist virtues, khanti-parami, which evokes a long-standing patience within the larger flow of life, a vow that allows us to accept that life and its currents are larger than our will, a patience that allows us to deepen our insight into our true nature and the nature of life.

So, the quick and slow work together, the sudden and all that unfolds over time inform each other. Like the crack of an egg, awakening can be quick, but like the cooking of that egg, understanding can take time.

While staying open to new experience, we're continually asked to practice forbearance: the art of waiting and withholding judgment until the lessons of our awakening take hold over time, becoming more and more clear.

The ancient Pali phrase *khanti-parami* encourages us "to bear praise and disdain with patience." This suggests that true understanding lives below the sway of our reactions to others and the reactions from others. We will feel the approval and rejection of others, because we're human, but the art of forbearance asks that we outwait the impact of approval and rejection, and our own judgment, until we can dive into the deeper waters of truth.

In our unending journey, we are like a great body of water: challenged to receive the stones thrown into us as they ripple and awaken our true nature (the work of kenshō) and then we are challenged to reflect on what has entered us, as it stirs up our bottom (the work of forbearance).

In the Middle East, the Aramaic word for heart, *lebak*, comes from a root that means "passion, courage, and vitality." It literally refers to "the heart or center of one's life." And the Sufi word for "inner consciousness" is *sirr*. Lebak and sirr—the consciousness of one's core.

This is where the work and practice of insight and patience live in us—in the consciousness of our core. It's the heart in concert with our mind that is the practice ground of our awakening and patience. It's in the live unfolding of our core that we learn how to dance with the quick and the slow, not choosing between the astonishment of insight or the curing of understanding over time. But letting us surface with the ancient face of innocence with which we can meet the world.

## *A Question to Walk With*

In your journal, describe a moment of direct insight that came to you, a moment of awakening that changed you. How did it present itself and what has it taught you about the nature of awakening? Later, in conversation with a friend or loved one, describe an understanding of life that has matured in your heart over time. How has this evolved and what has this taught you about the nature of understanding?

## Our Conversation Over Time

*Since we first saw a bison on the prehistoric plain and it seemed to stare back at us, we have unknowingly turned everything into us. With the curiosity of a child, we humanize everything—thinking the dog pouts when we are sad, thinking the bird is lighthearted when we are happy, thinking the cloud is lazy when we feel lost—all as a way to identify with the stream of life we find in everything we meet.*

*But all too often, we get enervated and lost in a lifetime of turning everything into us. We become a perceptual grinding mill, chewing up mystery after mystery through our self-centered gears until there's nothing left that doesn't resemble us.*

*All the while, the secret of the Universe resides in going the other way, in giving of ourselves to everything we meet in order to see and snort like a bison, to stretch and unfold like a flower, and to be clear and supple as a stream. The secret to the process of* yes *is to pour ourselves into everything we encounter, becoming what we meet.*

*Then, we can enter our days with the embodied feel of the common stuff of life.*

*Then, we can feel the river of life in our palms and realize that, though everything is different, everything is wonderfully the same on the inside. And it's from that immutable shimmer of being that we try, again and again, to utter small words that will remind us of this wonder when we forget. This shimmer of being that unifies everything without changing our uniqueness is at the heart of all our efforts to speak and name.*

## A WORD CLUSTER

namaste
neshama yetherah
perceive
receive

The Hindi word *namaste* means, "I bow to the portion of Universal Spirit that resides in you." In the West, we call the portion of Universal Spirit that lives in us our soul. The word *namaste* is first mentioned in the ancient Hindu scripture the *Rigveda* (1500 BC), indicating reverence and adoration. Sociologist Holly Oxhandler describes the word as meaning "the sacred in me recognizes the sacred in you."

This ancient greeting affirms our kinship with everything. It helps us recognize the flow of life, which never dies, as it moves through all the very tender forms that carry it. It helps us remember that Spirit is the electricity that animates all life. Being human, we trip and get tangled as soon as we step out of bed. And so, we can easily feel muffled and drift away from how precious everything is. To acknowledge the portion of Universal Spirit we each carry drops us under the web of circumstance and opinion, so we can meet each other authentically, one more time, with nothing in the way.

The greeting *namaste* is akin to the call and response of the African Bushmen, "I See You! I Am Here!" For centuries, the Bushmen have affirmed each other with resolve. When one becomes aware of his brother or sister coming out of the bush after hunting or gathering, the one at home exclaims, "I See You!" and then the one returning rejoices, "I Am Here!"

This timeless gesture of bearing witness is both simple and profound. We all need to be seen and heard, recognized and verified. This is the emotional lifeblood of all relationship, which in our busyness and pain we often forget. The wholehearted acknowledgment of each other's journey is at the heart of all therapy.

The greeting *namaste* is also akin to Martin Buber's restorative notion of I and Thou, which suggests that when we regard each other as two authentic living centers, God appears as the unrehearsed dialogue between us.

When we see ourselves as the sun and everyone we meet as planets in our orbit, we are trapped in the I–It relationship, objectifying everyone we meet. But when we can meet others as equal living beings, each with their own center, then we live out the I and Thou relationship, through which the Mystery of Universal Spirit manifests as a vital life-force between us.

Can you say namaste, then, quietly and with reverence, as you move through your day, stopping at the smallest sign of life, to let it in? Can you say "I See You!" to life wherever you meet it? Can you say "I Am Here!" wherever you go? Can you regard all that you meet as equally alive as you?

In truth, everyone struggles to stay awake and to remember how precious and rare everything is. In order to remediate the ways we lose concern, the Jews of Eastern Europe encouraged a daily taste of holiness. They believed that living keenly, openly, and authentically enlivened what they called the *neshama yetherah*, "the additional soul"; the soul below that restores the soul in the world.

All this implies that our movement between numbness and wakefulness is an unavoidable part of being human, a cycle we move through again and again. Once we accept this rhythm of closing and opening, we can recognize the signs of going to sleep as well as the signs of waking up. This is the art of the additional soul: to stay devoted to what will put us to sleep and what will wake us.

It's interesting that the word *perceive* and the word *receive* have the same Latin root, *percipere*, which means "to understand," from *per* which means "entirely" and *capere* which means "to take." To perceive, then, means "to take things in entirely, completely, in a way that covers us with understanding."

But to truly perceive, we must put down our screens and filters. In meeting life, we often block the true gift of perception by sorting things before they reach us, diluting their lessons. We often sort experience prematurely into things we believe or not, into things we see as true or false, into things we trust or distrust, into things we claim matter or things we claim don't matter.

All the while, the gift of perception resides in sustaining our unfiltered sensitivity to wonder, which means that, while we can always learn from others, we're called to be touched by life directly. We're called to maintain our firsthand experience, which then can be integrated with the experience of others. For true perception takes place below all the values and maps we inherit. True perception brings us closer to the life we're in while grounding us in the unfathomable life that holds us all.

## *A Question to Walk With*

In your journal, describe one circumstance or activity that puts your soul to sleep. Then, describe one circumstance or activity that wakes your soul up. How can you lean more into wakefulness than numbness? Later, in conversation with a friend or loved one, discuss the ways you can practice perceiving, that is, the ways you can "take things in entirely, completely, in a way that covers you with understanding."

## Our Conversation Over Time

*Over a lifetime, I've been given many names: poet, philosopher, teacher, seeker, cancer survivor. Yet who I am and what passes through me are larger and deeper than any one name. For the lifeblood of our identity flows like a waterfall. It can't be bottled. Though it's true that these names help me remember who I am when I'm lost. Like markers along the bend of a mountain that keep the wanderer on his way.*

### A WORD CLUSTER

person
so po
sant
shekinah
teacher

Being and becoming take time, and our commitment to stay open is at the very core of what it means to be a person. *Person*, from the Greek *per son*, means "the sound that passes through." And the Blackfoot word for wind is *so po*—"something going through." These simple yet profound notions seem to name our time on Earth. For something is always going through—from inner to outer, or the other way around. Like it or not, ready or not, it's this constant passage of life through us that forms us inwardly.

No matter how we protest, life keeps coming, and we can't

stop the invisible, imperfect river of time and its cleansings that scour us into who we are. Underneath our particular cuts and disappointments at how the dream of life has unfolded, underneath the way loneliness tastes to each of us, we are all formed by the same unseeable force of life passing through. It is the passing through of life that makes us a person. Ultimately, we are conduits, not containers. We are inlets, not quarries.

Eventually, every person must let life through by being thorough and real. This brings us to the history of the word *saint*, which didn't mean one who is pure and canonized. The original definition derived from the Sanskrit *sant*, meaning "truth seeker"—one who is fully alive, not perfect, but thorough and devoted to their own process of discovery; one whose greatness of soul is determined by their union with God's Being. This is our constant challenge: to honor and inhabit that Oneness of Being. In this, each of us is a saint—a truth seeker formed by the Oneness of Being that passes through us.

The question arises, again: How much of being a person is the result of our singular life and how much arises from the life of relationship? *Shekinah* is the Yiddish name for the indwelling face of God. Like a seed that stays dormant until it is watered, the indwelling face of God stays dormant in each person until watered with the nutrients of relationship. Toward such an end, Eastern European rabbis would ring a bell at dawn crying out, "Shekinah! The face of God is in exile!" Not exiled as in cast out, but exiled in the sense that

God is dormant until brought into the world through our relationships. So, in essence, the rabbis were saying, "Get up and Relate! And bring God into the World!" The rabbis were saying, "God is hidden until we love each other! God is waiting for you to relate His Essence into the world!"

As letting everything through is at the heart of being a person, revealing everything hidden is at the heart of being a teacher. In English, the word *teacher* goes back to Old English, meaning "to show or point out." The word *teacher* is related to the word *token*, which means "a visible or tangible representation of a fact, quality, or feeling." And so, the long history of teaching is deeply embedded in the vow to be a window to all that matters. Toward that end, teaching has always relied on the art of demonstration. The greatest teachers offer examples, not instructions. The greatest teachers lead students to their teacher within.

Regardless of subject matter, teaching is a noble ferrying between the shores of knowing and not knowing. In this way, each particular field of knowledge is a facet of the unknowable prism that is the Mystery of Life. And each field of knowledge serves as a way to manifest truth in the world—letting such being and truth move through us.

Across history, education has always been concerned with discovering meaning and building tools from that meaning, so we can learn how to use them. And the original words that reveal inwardness and the original words that show us how to live—they are instruments of being and care that will allow us to build or repair anything.

## *A Question to Walk With*

If to be a person is to be a conduit and not a container, then, in your journal, describe the state of your personhood as a conduit. Is your personhood clear and open or clogged and in need of repair? And what's coming through? Later, in conversation with a friend or loved one, discuss the part of you that needs to be brought alive through relationship. How can you enliven that part of your self more completely?

# The Journey of Inwardness

*In the New Testament, it's famously recorded that "In the beginning was the Word, and the Word was with God, and the Word was God." There are several orthodox interpretations of this. But a more foundational reading is that expression has always been the conduit between the essence of life and the experience of life. Expression has always been the way we connect inner and outer worlds.*

*But how did we go from uttering sounds to forming words to understanding the meaning such utterances convey? There are many theories for how we became capable of language that carries meaning. Rather than see them as alternatives, I offer them as thoughtful conjectures that together constellate a holistic understanding of the miracle of language.*

*In the 1700s, the German philosopher Johann Gottfried Herder saw early words as imitations of the cries of animals and birds. In 1861, the historical linguist Max Müller described our early utter-*

*ances as emotional exclamations and interjections triggered by our experiences such as pain, pleasure, confusion, and surprise.*

*And In 1871, Charles Darwin supported both Herder and Müller when he said:*

> I cannot doubt that language owes its origin to the imitation and modification, aided by signs and gestures, of various natural sounds, the voices of other animals, and man's own instinctive cries.

*Much earlier, medieval Muslim scholars of the Islamic Golden Age claimed that an inborn relationship exists between our expressions and the things they signify. So, language innately connects us to other life and emerges out of our human inclination to imitate the sounds and presence of nature.*

*It's also clear that, in addition to imitating the sounds and rhythms of the natural world, we also imitate the world of the mind and the world of feelings. Renaissance philosopher Antoine Arnauld proposed that people, being social and rational by nature, are drawn to weave language as a way to communicate the world of their ideas to each other.*

*From a primal point of view, the contemporary anthropologist Dean Falk has offered her "putting down the baby" theory, whereby a vocal call and response evolved between early human mothers and infants and this exchange led, eventually, to our earliest human words. Falk theorizes that early human mothers could not move around and forage with their infants clinging to them. In order to survive, Falk says:*

> These early mothers had to put their babies down. As a result, these babies needed to be reassured that they were not being abandoned. Mothers responded by developing "motherese"—an infant-directed communicative system embracing facial expressions, body language, touching, patting, caressing, laughter, tickling, and emotionally expressive contact calls.

*The cognitive scientist Philip Lieberman had another theory for our ability to traffic in speech with meaning. He proposed that we differ from animals in our ability to speak because, over the eons, our larynx or voice box descended while our tongue remained horizontal in the oral cavity. This gave us the lingual dexterity to evolve a more sophisticated phonation than animals. Lieberman suggests that, in time, this evolutionary shift in our biology enabled civilization to unfold.*

*Underlying all this is the mystical sense that language is endlessly indicative of a larger Unity that exists beyond the realm of words but which is humbly pointed to by any form of authentic speech.*

*In Sanskrit, the goddess Vac is a personified form of unitive speech, a residual aspect of Spirit. She is the mother of all Vedas (the anonymous Hindu scriptures), and the mother of all emotions and the friend of all musicians. Another way to describe Vac is as the energy or light that animates each of us when we open our heart fully to life. In this way, language can be understood as a discharge of unified energy that courses through a human being, using that life as an instrument.*

*In Greek mythology, the word* muse *refers to each of the nine goddesses who are the source of artistic inspiration in human beings.*

*Both the spark of Vac and the call of the muses fill the human voice with song, fill the human body with dance, and lift the human mind the way wind lifts a wing. The presence and guidance of Vac and the muses are considered the source of all language.*

*There is no reason to have to choose between these offerings, which themselves come to us through the miracle of thought and feeling and language. Together, they point to the inexplicable dynamic that allows us to see each other through the fog and say, "Though I don't yet know you, we are of the same tribe."*

*This chapter explores the words and phrases that help us find our way to the groundings of Spirit that let us make our way in the world.*

## A WORD CLUSTER

### insight

Despite what we've been taught, intelligence is not our sole authorship of ideas, but the ongoing relationship between the part and the Whole from which ideas are the trail. Beyond our tiny self, intelligence is the ongoing quest of a note to find its place in a symphony written by time as we go. The other day, a flock of birds appeared. Suddenly, they all veered right in unison. Since their brains are so small, what form of innate intelligence guides them to move in response to the wind and to each other? We need to be this agile. But as long as we think intelligence begins and ends with us, we will never find it, enter it, or dance with it.

When we approach intelligence as a form of relationship

through which we might better know the Universe and navigate life, we can better understand the original meaning of the word *insight*.

We typically assume that the word *insight* refers to a culminating or incisive understanding, a crystallization that comes from our experience. And it is. However, the original meaning of insight is "to see from within." Insight refers to the *place* from which we see as well as what we *distill* from what we see. While both are important, we need to consider the place from which we see *before* concluding anything, because the place from which we make conclusions is often diminished or tinted or limited to begin with.

If we see everything through glasses that are dark, our conclusion will be that we live in a dark world. To see clearly, the practice of insight requires that we *restore* ourselves to a place of depth and breadth, re-establishing a more fundamental and encompassing vantage point that lets us truly see. This can change everything.

## *A Question to Walk With*

Sit quietly and consider the place from which you see and settle there. In your journal, describe that place within and then look at yourself, your life, and the world from this inner vantage point. Consider a problem and a joy from this place of seeing within. What do you notice? Note the path to and from this essential place so you can return.

## A WORD CLUSTER

aikido
confidence
self-confidence
courage

Though the word *aikido* describes a modern Japanese martial art, the word itself translates as "the way of unifying [with] life energy." And so, the dynamics of aikido can serve as an oath of perception through which to meet our days—to always look for how we can unify with what we encounter while doing no harm.

Based on the ancient martial art jujutsu and the Oomoto religious tradition, aikido was created by Morihei Ueshiba with the aim to create a practice by which individuals can defend themselves while keeping their attackers safe from injury. It's important to note that the Oomoto religious tradition promotes harmony by returning to the interwoven relationships that were at work in the "Great Origin."

Aikido is also known as "the way of harmonious spirit." The word itself is comprised of three parts: *ai* which means "combine, unite, join together"; *ki* which means "energy or force"; and *do* which means "a way or practice." Therefore, aikido represents, more broadly, "the way and practice of combining forces."

How, then, can you organize and inhabit your life in such a way as to combine the forces of life without causing injury to those you meet? How can you enliven the interwoven relationships that were at work in the Great Origin of the Universe? How can you work to join and not separate, to unify and not divide, so you can meet the days with rhythm and not dissonance?

One way to stay centered in the flow of life's forces is to practice self-confidence, which is not the art of puffing yourself up or masquerading as something other than you are. If we look more closely at the word *confidence*, we can trace it back to its Indo-European root *bheidh*, which means "to trust and abide." The word *restore* means "to bring back to life." Restoring confidence then has something to do with "bringing our trust back to life."

It is helpful to note psychologist Michael Mahoney's definition of *self-confidence*. He traces *confidence* to the Latin *confidere* which means "fidelity." And so, he frames self-confidence as a fidelity to the true self, staying faithful and devoted to the journey of our evolving inner life. Indeed, it is our devotion to that sacred journey beneath our endless moods that brings us back in accord with the center of the heart, which shares the same living center with all beings. This is what the Hindu tradition calls *atman*, "the shared immortal self."

So, confidence is not the swagger or certainty that we convey to the world. It's the fidelity with which we listen to and relate to the irreducible foundation of all life.

The work of self-confidence, then, is to stay committed to both the work of integrity and the work of compassion:

honoring the real experience of others and ourselves while honoring the continuous flow of life that exists beneath our experience. Through the work of integrity and the work of compassion, self-confidence becomes the practice of fidelity to the true and shared immortal self.

This brings us to the original definition of the word *courage*, which comes from the Latin *cor*, which literally means "heart." But the original use of the word *courage* means "to stand by one's core." Discovering this original idiom for courage was the doorway for me to retrieve my book *Finding Inner Courage.*

In everyday terms, when we can stand by our core, we discover our own authority of being. By doing so, we are aligned with the authority of all being. This restores and sustains our self-confidence, our fidelity to the journey of our true self, which, in turn, helps us to combine the forces of life without doing harm. All this—to live in accord with the life around us and the life within us.

## *A Question to Walk With*

In your journal, describe your experience with self-confidence as your fidelity to the journey of your inner self. Later, in conversation with a friend or loved one, discuss the particular ways that you can work with life's forces without doing harm to others.

## Our Conversation Over Time

*The gall wasp lays her eggs on the bud of an oak leaf and begins to form a shell-like chamber from which, in time, the mother wasp eats its way out. The hardened shell, also known as a gall, is somewhere between the size of a marble and a walnut. For centuries, the remnants of the hollowed gall have been harvested for its tannins which, when mixed with iron sulfate, create the purple-black ink known as oak gall ink. This was the standard writing ink used throughout the world until the twentieth century.*

*An early recipe for the ink goes back to Pliny the Elder of Rome. Many of Leonardo da Vinci's drawings were made using oak gall ink. And legendary documents such as the Magna Carta and the American Declaration of Independence were written with oak gall ink.*

*It's not by accident that the ink with which human beings have declared their freedom is made from the residue of a small creature who can only begin its life of flight by eating its way out of its own shell. This parallels the journey ordinary souls must make to truly be free in the world: forming in the dark of our own single chamber, only to eat our way out of our hardened shell, leaving the ink of freedom behind.*

### A WORD CLUSTER

disrobe
effort

During the pandemic, I worked online with a large group of students in China. It was a five-week course and the whole process was a gift. To prepare for the sessions, I worked very closely with Joy Huang Xiaoyu, whose depth of understanding in both Chinese and English is remarkable. As my translator, she guided us through a beautiful journey, unraveling words to the very fiber of their meaning.

I wanted to open one of the sessions with a poem of mine called "Disrobing in Time." The poem affirms that the only power we have when feeling powerless is to admit the truth of our experience. By this act of acceptance, we disrobe ourselves of all excuses and denials until we stand naked in our truth.

Joy quickly asked, "What do you mean by *disrobe*?" After discussing the poem in more detail, Joy exclaimed, "We have a perfect word for this!" Then, she introduced me to the Chinese word 蜕变 (tuh-way be-yan), which means "taking off all coverings to become one's true self as time unfolds." The ideogram literally means a snake taking off its skin to find its new skin, or a caterpillar breaking through its cocoon to become a butterfly. The word implies growth and transformation.

I was stunned at the depth and breadth of this one word. We have no such word in English. The Chinese word serves as a threshold. It reveals a theme, a vow, a practice central to living an awakened life: How do we take off all our coverings to become our true self as time unfolds? In essence, this question is at the heart of all my work. For this is how we endure and remain more than what is done to us. This long, slow gesture that lives between effort and grace is at the center of all inner practice.

This brings us to the word *effort*, which combines the Latin prefix *ex*, meaning "to extract or express," with another Latin word, *fortis*, which means "strong." So effort of the deepest nature is the act of extracting or expressing strength. The Dutch word for *effort* means "inspanning." So effort also implies the work of spanning or bridging distances.

This is the work we are returned to, over and again: to span distances and bridge differences in order to take off the coverings that keep us from becoming our true self. This is how a soul becomes itself across its decades on Earth. What do these deep notions mean to you personally? How can you release your soul through your continual effort to take off what is unnecessary, so your true self can unfold?

## *A Question to Walk With*

In your journal, describe one particular effort you can make to span the distance between what you show the world and what you show yourself. Then, describe one particular effort you can make to bridge a difference between you and another. Later, in conversation with a friend or loved one, discuss your journey to this point in your life in taking off all coverings in order to become your true self.

## Our Conversation Over Time

*There is always a mystery to words that describe what is intangible. Words—like* love, loss, truth, Spirit, *and* peace*—always have a taste of what is beyond them. Imagine dipping a cup into a river. What you* *drink from that cup is just a small part of what filled the cup. Words that carry deep meaning are like this. They always carry something from a deeper source.*

*The Australian singer, songwriter, and poet Nick Cave speaks about the same quality in song lyrics:*

> Many of my favorite lyrics are those that I do not fully understand. They seem to exist in a world of their own—in a place of potentiality, adjacent to meaning. The words feel authentic or true, but remain mysterious, as if a greater truth lies just beyond our understanding. I see this, not just within a song, but within life itself, where awe and wonder live in the tension between what we understand and what we do not understand.

*In this way, all that we know is, indeed, a small glimpse of all that we don't know. In this way, we're asked not to confine our exploration to what we already know, but to keep living at the edge of what we know. This is how we meet each other at the deepest level. This next set of words explores the qualities and conditions that help us inquire at the edge of what we know.*

## A WORD CLUSTER

hsien
inscape
insearch
intuit

The Chinese word *hsien* means "profound serenity and quietness." It immediately conjures a sense of stillness, the aim of all meditation, through which we can see and feel the world around us and within us more clearly.

The ideogram for this word renders the moon shining through an open gate or a tree standing alone within the gates of a courtyard. These root images suggest that the deep being of life will both penetrate us, opening the gates we create, and exist within us, despite the gates we keep closed. For being—like the moon and the tree—ignores gates, opened or closed.

Stillness makes the world around us and within us transparent, the way a still patch of water reveals the bottom of a lake. In just this way, being still enough lets the truth of things show through the agitation of the surface. When we visit the bottom of things that always exists beneath the agitation of circumstance, we start to realize that being has a landscape all its own. When we can be still enough long enough, we inhabit a way of being that allows us to map the foundation of life. This is the practice of hsien.

Expressed in another way, the British poet Gerard Manley Hopkins coined the term *inscape* to refer to the inner landscape of life. And the great Chilean poet Pablo Neruda talked about becoming so intimate with the inscape of being and the outer landscape of the world that he would, in time, become a student of the geography of self.

In everyday terms, the waking life involves the art of breaking trail and mapping the interior. By staying devoted to learning more and more about the inscape of being and how it informs the landscape of the world, we partake in the humbling journey referred to in the ancient Lakota saying "The longest journey you will make in your life is from your head to your heart."

Not long because we are slow or incompetent, but long because the distance between our head and our heart is a vast continent that takes years to cross.

To land in our heart and live an embodied life requires a commitment, both inwardly and outwardly, beyond what we already know. Outwardly, there's always the need to gather more information in order to know what is possible. This is called research. But just as important is our need for *insearch*, the time needed to know what is true and immutable in the deepest context.

In addition to reason, the quality of intuition is a great tool by which to do insearch into the depth of living. The word *intuit* means "to look upon, to instruct from within, to understand or learn by instinct." And *instinct* refers to "a learning we are born with." So intuition is the very personal way we listen to the Universe in order to discover and rediscover the learnings we are born with. As such, intuition is a deep form of listening that when trusted can return us to the common, irrepressible element at the center of all life. Intuition can help us move through the agitation of circumstance to the still bottom of things where the sensation of Oneness surrounds us.

To keep learning both inwardly and outwardly and to braid their lessons is at the heart of resilience.

## *A Question to Walk With*

In your journal, describe where you are in your journey from your head to your heart. Later, in conversation with a friend or loved one, discuss the understanding you each have about the inner landscape (or inscape) of being. Describe your favorite place to visit inwardly and why.

## A WORD CLUSTER

nekkhamma-parami
paradox
radical
respect
remember

One of the ten Buddhist virtues, nekkhama-parami, invokes a renunciation of all that is not essential, a vow to discern want from need so we can make a practice of shedding what entangles us. In order to create such a practice, we have to inhabit the original notion of what it means to meet paradox, what it means to be radical, what it means to respect, and what it truly means to remember.

*Paradox* means "beyond belief," from the Greek *para* ("beyond") and *dox* ("belief"). "Beyond belief" means more than *unbelievable*, but rather beyond our current understanding of things. Engaging paradox, then, is crucial because, without the courage and patience to listen beyond what we already know—without the ability to outlast the map of our opinions—we are never baptized into the full depth of life.

In an experiential way, paradox can also be understood as any moment where more than one thing is true at the same time. And paradox can jar us from our myopic opinions into a deeper logic of Spirit where all things are true. It's this deeper listening to the many sides of truth that allows us to root ourselves in the Mystery of Life, which can help us endure the harsh weather of life.

This leads us to the word *radical*. In the political realm, people are considered radical when they advocate complete social or political change. Yet there is a more foundational meaning of the word, which comes from the Latin *radicalis*, meaning "inherent, forming the root."

In the plant world, *radical* means "return to the root." And the word *respect* means "to look again." A *radical respect*, therefore, means "to return with open eyes to the root of things." In its deepest sense, to be radical is not veering sharply from the norm but pursuing and returning to the intrinsic nature of things.

This speaks to something very essential in being alive. For, in order to renunciate all that is not essential, in order to disentangle ourselves from the map of our opinions, we are constantly asked to return with open eyes to the root of things.

All this works in concert with the meaning of the word *remember*, which is much more than the conjuring of nostalgia.

Rather, to remember is to put the members back together in order to make what is broken and separated whole again. So, the true purpose of memory is to excavate the past in order to become whole.

How, then, can you make sense of your past in a way that makes you whole? And from such regained wholeness, how can you put down the map of your opinions? And once whole and free of your hardened ways of thinking and feeling, how can you return with open eyes to the root of things? To engage these vows in a personal way is what it means to renunciate all that is not essential. It is how the heart scours the patina of experience that covers the mind.

## *A Question to Walk With*

In your journal, describe one way you're entangled in the map of your own opinions and one way you can return with open eyes to the root of things. Later, in conversation with a friend or loved one, discuss a paradox you are struggling with and what it's trying to teach you.

## Our Conversation Over Time

*I wonder, who was the first to voice the word* pain? *After eons of prehistoric cries and moans, very much like the grunts of animals, when was this singular and bottomless word first uttered by humans? And how does naming it soften our experience of pain? I only know that acute pain can make us forget that life is a blessing. And yet, the long weight of pain can drop us into the most tender state of blessing. I think we need many words for* pain, *the way Eskimos have a myriad of words for* snow. *Perhaps the evermore subtle naming of pain and how we can share it will let us rediscover, when real enough and tender enough, that, no matter the difficulty, it is a rare privilege to be here at all.*

## A WORD CLUSTER

root
sage
sincere

The base definition of the word *root* is very helpful. A root is defined as "the part of a thing that attaches it to a greater, more fundamental whole." The root of a tree or flower attaches itself to the soil from which all trees and flowers grow. And the self, if planted deeply, is a root that attaches our singular journey to the greater, archetypal journey that all life goes through. In these terms, we can think of our individual soul as a root that attaches the life of a person to the greater, more fundamental life of Spirit. In essence, the very words we're exploring in this book are roots to the ground of meaning and life-force that help us live.

How, then, do we extend our life as a root? How do we keep all our parts connected to the Whole of Life? Two enduring ways are by tasting life directly and by the release of our sincerity.

So, it's no mistake that the word *sage* comes from the Latin *sapere* ("to taste"). In its original form, *sage* is a verb, a process or gesture by which we take in the world. It implies that we make sense of the world and find wisdom by tasting. While watching and thinking may be helpful, it's internalizing what we experience that opens us to wisdom.

In ancient Greece, we can trace a fundamental shift in the meaning of wisdom and our approach to it. In that society, *sage* begins to refer to someone who *has* tasted, who has internalized the world and its many paradoxes. While we can certainly learn from such individuals, a significant change takes place that alters how we understand learning when the focus becomes the one who has tasted and not the practice of tasting itself.

When the word *sage* became a noun, a middleman was inserted who, till this day, expounds to others how they should live. Now there's the misguided belief that we can shortcut the process of *saging* and receive wisdom through one already wise.

Nonetheless, the instruction of true sages throughout time has been to redirect seekers back to their own innate resources and firsthand experiences of the world. For the only way to attach ourselves to the greater Whole of Life is through the sustained process of saging, which is tasting life directly.

The most essential and enduring quality that keeps us

ever engaged in life directly is the effort of our sincerity. The ancient Chinese text *The Doctrine of the Mean* comforts us by saying, "Given sincerity, there will be enlightenment." This affirms the quiet truth that only through our complete presence of welcome can we experience the strength and beauty of the Universe and the peace that connects all living things. Only by being sincere can we taste life directly. Only through a sincere life can we know love and compassion. Only by devoting ourselves to sincerity can we know God.

But to understand the practice of sincerity, we need to look at the more human side of its meaning, which originated in Rome. If we trace the Western form of the word, it comes from the Latin *sin cere*, which means "without wax."

During the Italian Renaissance, sculptors were as plentiful as plumbers, and markets selling marble and other stones were as prevalent as hardware stores. As in any age, there were those ready to deceive. And fraudulent stone sellers would frequently fill the cracks in flawed stones with wax and try to sell them as flawless. Thus, an honest stone seller became known as someone who was *sincere*—one who showed his stone, without wax, cracks and all.

A sincere person then referred to someone who is honest and open enough not to hide their flaws. This honest stance becomes even more important when we consider, as the Jungian priest John Malecki said, that "without vulnerability, there can be no transformation." For it's by and through our humanness that we grow and change and are allowed to transform. Without the places cracked and softened by experience and time, we remain too hard and fixed to be affected by life.

In Tibetan mythology, it's said that a spiritual warrior, one committed to a life of transformation, always has a crack in their heart. Because that's how the Mysteries get in.

So, if we're to stay enlivened by attaching ourselves to a greater, more fundamental Whole (to be a root), we must find a way to taste life directly (to practice saging). And we must be sincere. We must live in the open, flaws and all, so that the Mysteries have a way to enter us and fill us with the power of life—one more time.

### *A Question to Walk With*

In your journal, describe a crack in your heart and how it changed your life. Later, in conversation with a friend or loved one, discuss how you experience the process of saging, of tasting of life directly.

## Our Conversation Over Time

*We spend so much time anthropomorphizing other life. That is, we attribute human characteristics to all we encounter. As I mentioned earlier, we tend to turn everything we see into us. At first, this is endearing, a way to move closer to things. But unless we let other life inform us, such projection diminishes the great diversity of life, only letting it get close if it stays like us. In time, we can become inexorable and intransigent, unwilling to accept anything different from us.*

*The antidote to this insidious narcissism is to let other life in and to learn from other ways of being, so we can add to what it means to be human. Here's a poem of mine that speaks to my own struggle with this:*

INHABITING WONDER

If the sun thinks
by radiating light,
its language is warmth.

If the ocean thinks
by undulating its mass of waves,
its language is wetness.

If a tree thinks
by converting light to sugar,
its language
is the sprouting of leaves.

If the wind thinks
by moving unseen
through everything,
how it bends us
is its tongue.

I am tired
of only thinking like a man
and pray for the courage

to radiate, undulate, sprout,
and move through
everything
unseen.

*How, then, does a stone speak of endurance? Certainly not with words, but by its complete is-ness. And how does water pray? Not with words as we know them, but by surrendering to the flow of life that carries it. What words, then, can we create to help us understand complete is-ness and what it means to surrender to flow? This is the lasting medicine of words: how to take the various currents of life and give voice to them in a way that lets us imbibe their life-force when we need it.*

## A WORD CLUSTER

makoto
yūgen
oku
hanamuke

I want to explore a constellation of Japanese words that speak profoundly to the life of our inwardness. *Makoto* is a Japanese word meaning "truth, reality, and sincerity." The word signifies the bare, unadorned truth of things as they are. It's used to refer to any person, thought, feeling, or object that is not covered or tainted by anything false. It's a Japanese tradition to name a child Makoto in the hope that the life of that child will be lived beneath all falseness.

Such a commitment to eschew what is false leads us to the well of meaning that inwardness opens. For it's through our constant journey of inwardness that we stay close to a life that is true.

The Japanese word *yūgen* means "a depth and mystery of meaning" in which "beauty [is] only partially perceived, fully felt but barely glimpsed by the viewer."

This is the nature of inwardness that our authenticity brings us to. And though we can feel both depth and mystery completely, we can only glimpse it partially with our mind. When we tread water in the ocean, we rise and fall, feeling the complete immersion that buoys us, though we can barely see what holds us up. Likewise, it's our immersion in inwardness that buoys us through the days, though the Wholeness of Life exists beyond our comprehension.

Alan Watts offers these examples of yūgen. When geese disappear into the clouds, we can't see them, though we know they are still there. And when looking at a mountain, we can't see the far side of the mountain, though we know it is there. Likewise, in moments of yūgen, the greater realms of existence that hold us are sensed and felt but not readily seen.

The medieval Japanese poet Chomei illustrates a moment of yūgen when he says: "On an autumn evening, for example, there is no color in the sky, nor any sound, and although we cannot give a definite reason for it, we are somehow moved to tears."

The Japanese word *oku* means "within"; more deeply "the interior" characterized by being "intimate, deep, and sacred." The word is famously used in the title of Basho's record of his walking pilgrimage around the island of Japan in 1689, *Oku no Hosomichi*, which translates as "Narrow Road to the Interior."

As spirits living in the world, we are ever wedded to the narrow road to the interior in order to gather meaning so we can live more completely without falseness in the world. This journey inward and back is how the awakened soul migrates through its time on Earth.

And what we bring back from the interior are the gifts we can't do without: peace, courage, tenderness, acceptance, generosity, and compassion. With this in mind, consider that the Japanese word *hanamuke* means "parting gifts" that are used in a farewell. It can also refer to gifts that are impossible to leave behind. The enduring qualities we bring back from the interior are indispensable gifts we can't live without. And returning to the world, we often feel compelled to share those gifts with others on their way.

Each of these Japanese words elicits a practice we can personalize. How can we uncover and discard falseness whenever it appears? How can we trust the depth we feel, even when its full comprehension eludes our mind? How can we make a practice of following our own narrow road to the interior? And, just as crucial, how can we commit to making our way back? Finally, what good is what we come back with, if we don't share it?

## *A Question to Walk With*

In your journal, describe a part of your journey that proved false. How did you realize it was false? How did you put down what proved false? How did you find a path more true? Later, in conversation with a friend or loved one, discuss your most recent road to the interior. What led you there? What did you discover in the interior? What did you bring back? What do you want to share from the interior with others?

## Our Conversation Over Time

*In the Old Testament, when God calls out to Moses through the burning bush on Mount Sinai, Moses answers without hesitation, "Hineni!" In Hebrew* hineni *means "Here I am. I am listening. I am available." In exclaiming hineni, the weary prophet offers himself as ready and available to whatever is asked of him.*

*This readiness to listen and be available to whatever life asks of us engages our spirit in a way that keeps us vital. For giving ourselves over completely to whatever is before us—whether it be suffering or wonder—is how we heal where we are broken or bereft. One of the great, enduring purposes of love and suffering is to drop us into the depth of life repeatedly until we meet the world from the restorative center of our being. This is the way of hineni.*

*Very often, the place from which we meet the world is from the tangle of circumstance we find ourselves in. When blessed to drop below that, we often settle into the stories we've been told about ourselves and life, as well as the narratives created by our wounds. In time, if blessed, we drop below both the tangle of circumstance and the tangle of our narratives. When we can stay committed to the way of hineni, uttering, "Here I am. I am listening. I am available," we can meet the world with unmitigated life-force.*

*To be sure, the life of circumstance and narrative never goes away, but living from the center of our being, they no longer define us. They move to the background of our consciousness. When we can commit to working with what we are given, declaring again and again, "Here I am. I am listening. I am available," our felt sense of original presence is restored, allowing us to become intimate with all things.*

## A WORD CLUSTER

trust
tawakkul
virgin

The word *trust* came into English about 1200 AD, meaning "to rely on the veracity of someone or something." This sense of reliance on truth goes back to the Old Norse word *traust* which means "strong." If we go back further, we find several derivatives of the word *trust*, all indicating places of firm foundation.

The Indo-European root of the word is *dreu*, which means "to be steadfast or solid," such as the density of wood in a solid tree. Variants of the root dreu include *true*, from the Old English *trēowe* which means "firm"; the Old French *triste* which means "waiting place"; and the Celtic word *druwid* which means "a strong seer."

So, in its original sense, the word *trust* constellates to mean: that which is steadfast and firm, evoking a veracity that will make us a strong seer. And strong seeing will lead us to the waiting place where we can rest in what is lasting and true. Ultimately, trust, in the deepest context, concentrates all the inner aspects needed to follow your heart.

For following and trusting your heart is central to finding what is true, the way having clear lungs is central to breathing. The practice of trust is central to sustaining an awakened life.

With this in mind, I offer four trusts that help us on our way:

- trust in the common presence in all things;
- trust in the fact that no matter how we are split, we will regenerate and heal;
- trust in the blessing that true intimacy will open us to Oneness;
- and trust that what churns up our bottom only deepens our flow.

These four trusts mark "the fullness of trust in God," which Sufis call tawakkul.

I ask you, then, how do these four trusts appear in your life? Which are your strengths? Which need more attention? What is your history with the four trusts? When have you been aware of the presence in all things and what has that felt like? In what ways have you witnessed or experienced the mysterious process of regeneration? Tell the story of a "split that has grown back."

And how has true intimacy deepened your experience of life? By intimacy, I mean more than sex, but rather the safe truth-telling space that unfolds between two human beings when the humility in being alive opens the heart's eye.

I also invite you to tell the story of a time when life churned up your bottom, how that felt, and how, when the disturbance settled, you were deeper for it. If you haven't experienced these forms of trust, search for them and talk about them. For entering the questions and telling our stories call the four trusts to our side, the way native chants invite the corn to grow.

In truth, the four trusts keep opening us to life. For me, the doorway to my work as a poet was shut until I could accept the common presence in all things. And cancer taught me to surrender to however life might churn up my bottom. I am here to say that, after much painful churning, my masks dissolved and my flow has deepened. And in the days that remain, I keep learning how true intimacy—the art of facing and receiving the full humanity of one another—is a blessing that leads us to what is lasting and true.

I only know that taking the risk to follow my heart lets me swim in the four trusts until I stop hesitating to love which, in turn, gives me access to the very fabric of life. I only know that, without such trust, we can turn blunt and cruel.

At the heart of it, that we will fall and fail and make mistakes is not newsworthy. It's in facing what we've done or failed to do that our character is formed. It's in what we choose to lean on and trust when getting up that lets us begin again. I only know that when face down, I've heard the Universe whisper: If you could only settle into the silence beneath your fear, you'd come alive and simply hold each other.

I only know that once committed to following your heart, the things of the world, seen and unseen, begin to speak. This is the conversation we long for. This is the conversation that lets beauty come through all the suffering, the way light filters through a canopy of branches to warm the forest floor.

And when we trust, we offer an ease of life to each other. This is the way of true friends. For those who follow their heart will want you to be yourself before anything else. Then, friendship is the safest harbor. As the kind Irish poet John O' Donohue said, "A friend . . . awakens your life in order to free the wild possibilities within you."

Add to all this the fact that the word *virgin* originally referred to a woman who is faithful unto herself. Originally, beneath the word's sexual connotation, to be virginal speaks to our fidelity to a core sense of self, beneath the pressures and opinions of others. This fidelity to who we are, in spite of others, is the beginning of our friendship with the Universe. It's from this place of enduring trust that we can begin to experience the common presence in all things. It's from this deep waiting place that we can begin to know the blessing of true intimacy.

## *A Question to Walk With*

In your journal, describe a moment when you felt the common presence in all things. How did this presence reach you and how did it touch you? Later, in conversation with a friend or loved one, discuss your history of deep trust, where you have found it and where you have felt betrayed. Discuss your personal definition of trust and how you can strengthen your trust in life.

# The Nature of Life

*This chapter explores words that speak to the nature of life itself. Most traditions refer to life in its Mysterious Wholeness as an all-encompassing, unseeable current that carries us all. We are often so preoccupied with the choppiness of life on our raft that we seldom try to understand the Ocean of Mystery that lifts us and surrounds us. A greater knowledge of these currents can make the journey less choppy.*

## A WORD CLUSTER

inochi
inspire
luglio
viaticum
manna
mana

In Japanese, the word *inochi* means "the life-essence that is in everything." This life-essence knits us together and keeps us together. Another name for this life-essence is Spirit, which reveals itself in anything that is life-giving. As such, Spirit is in every breath.

And since *inspire* means "to inhale," it is by breathing in the life-essence around us that we are inspired, brought alive. In traditional Chinese medicine, the term *spiritual* is used to describe "anything that is life-giving." Our inner health resides in the exchange by which we take in life-essence and release it. What this looks like and feels like is very personal and particular, while its effect is universal. Regardless of how it looks or feels, the exchange of life-essence is life-giving. We each must stay devoted to this exchange. But how? By what means and practices can we devote ourselves to the exchange of life-essence?

This brings us to the Swahili word *luglio*, which means "food that you carry with you." In Latin, *viaticum* is a term that means "food along the way." It refers to the Eucharist offered as Communion in the Catholic Church. Both terms can refer to actual food, but they imply a deeper sort of food that can sustain the soul on its journey.

This leads us into the twin history of the words *manna* and *mana*. In the Old Testament, *manna* refers to the daily bread that fed the Jews while wandering the desert after leaving their bondage in Egypt. It had to be made daily or it would spoil.

Later, when Jesus said, "Give us this day our daily bread,"

he invoked a renewable form of sustenance. In this regard, manna implies a form of spiritual nourishment that has to be remade every day. Jesus spoke of manna as the daily inner food, the spiritual food that can sustain us, which has to be created daily. This speaks to how the daily practice of inwardness is necessary to stay integral and whole.

But earlier than these definitions is the Polynesian definition of *mana* that refers to the numinous quality of Spirit that emanates within everything: rock, river, bird, human, even a chair. This brings us full circle to the Japanese notion of inochi, the life-essence that is in everything.

Carl Jung later added his psycho-spiritual definition of mana as "the unconscious influence of one being on another." Jung put forth the notion that when we can be as present and authentic as the sun, then we will grow toward each other, exerting a form of spiritual gravity that exists at a more fundamental level than argument, debate, or persuasion.

How, then, can you open your self authentically to the life-essence that exists in everything? By what personal practices can you inspire yourself—that is, breathe in life-essence—so that it serves as your daily inner food?

## *A Question to Walk With*

In your journal, describe one form of inner food that you must renew every day in order to stay close to the life-essence that is in everything. How do you go about this process?

## Our Conversation Over Time

*When I was in graduate school, we were required to take a course called "The History and Structure of the English Language." Though everyone thought it would be a dry trek through anthropology and phonemes, it was fascinating and dynamic, largely because of Dr. George Hastings, a tall, thin, wide-eyed scholar with a long white beard.*

*He was explaining the great vowel shift that mysteriously took place over a three-hundred-year period between 1400 and 1700 AD. It seems to have started in southern England and affected all the dialects of English throughout the world. During this time, the placement of our tongue while pronouncing vowels shifted completely. For example, the pronunciation of "oo" became "oh" and the pronunciation of "too" became "toe." Imagine shifting the face of a clock so that when denoting twelve, the hour hand points to where three currently is, and when denoting three, the hour hand points to where six currently is, and so on.*

*This inexplicable shift in how Europeans spoke accounts for our migration from the Middle English that Chaucer spoke and wrote to the modern English that we speak and write today.*

*I remember raising my hand and asking Dr. Hastings what caused such a monumental shift? He smiled slowly and said, "If you put two rowboats, untied, next to each other in the ocean, you wouldn't expect them to be near each other the next day." He paused and continued, "Why would we expect the vessels of language to stay put?" Then, he leaned closer and added, "And it might happen again in another thousand years."*

*From that day on, I realized that language is dynamic and fluid, a network of living things akin to the swell of seas and the growth of forests.*

## A WORD CLUSTER

maya

In Hinduism, Maya is the goddess of illusion. The word *maya* refers to "the appearance of the surface world that covers the ultimate, underlying reality." It's believed that anything added to the truth of things as they are is illusion. This veiling power of illusion creates the differences known as "me" and "mine." In this way, maya creates the ignorance of the individual self that thinks it is separate from the rest of life. The unitive view of life that we are born with fragments into self-centered thinking by the layering of illusion. And so, we each must practice what the Hindus call parting the veil of illusion in order to stay close to what matters. How, then, can you practice parting your own veils of illusion in order to stay close to what matters?

## *A Question to Walk With*

In your journal, describe one aspect of separation that complicates your life and one aspect of the Unified Reality that restores your sense of connection. Later, in conversation with a friend or loved one, discuss the difference between separation and unity as you experience it from day to day.

## A WORD CLUSTER

mitakuye oyasin

We're not alone in this perennial task to be who we are and stay connected. Every spiritual path asserts that everything is connected through a net of influences that each path names differently. And every tradition acknowledges that it's our human challenge to hold on to this fundamental connection. The Native Americans are wise teachers of this, affirming and reaffirming that all things are related.

Consider the native phrase "all my relations" (from the Lakota *mitakuye oyasin*), which suggests that existence is a family of relationship, one animated thing influencing another. So deep is this notion that when members of the Blackfoot tribe greet each other, they do not say, "How are you?" but "How are the connections?" (*Tza Nee da Bee Wah?*). For how you are is embedded in your connections to everything that exists. If the connections are intact, then you are intact.

### *A Question to Walk With*

In your journal, describe your own web of connection, your own sense of *all my relations*, outlining which connections are strong and which are frayed. How can you begin to strengthen the connections that are frayed?

## A WORD CLUSTER

### naturalangsamkeit

*Naturalangsamkeit* is a German word that means "the slowness of natural development." Often, it's the speed of the modern world that separates us from our underlying kinship with all things. Often, it's the urgency with which we hurry through life that tangles us in the veil of illusion. Often, it's how we run through life that makes us feel isolated and severed from the Native American sense that all things are related.

But regardless of how advanced and quick we are in so many directions at once, things that matter, wonderfully, still take time. So much depends on the slowness of natural development. So much depends on the long view of time.

We are so trained to want results and conclusions immediately that we seldom allow the truth of things to unfold. I have been humbled to voice poems along the way, only to discover years later that they are part of something larger and deeper that I couldn't have foreseen.

Often, it's the slowness of natural development that humbles us into compassion and acceptance, as only the passage of time will allow us to inhabit a position we long criticized or judged. Only when I've finally fallen do I have compassion for how others have stumbled. Only when I've experienced loss can I understand how tightly others have held on to what or who they so dearly loved. Blessed are those who can outwait their own judgment.

### *A Question to Walk With*

In conversation with a friend or loved one, discuss one thing that has taken a long time to blossom within you. How has your understanding of this quality changed over time?

## Our Conversation Over Time

*In the Aztec culture of Central America, the beginning of language comes from a story in which only Coxcox and his wife, Xochiquetzal, survive the Great Flood by taking refuge in the hollow of a cypress tree that carries them on the water to the clearing on a great mountain. There, they start again and have many children, all of whom are mute. After many years, it's believed that the Great Spirit took pity on them and sent a dove who placed a seed in each child's dream as they slept. And since each child watered the seed in their dream with the unique feelings of their heart, each child awoke speaking a different language.*

*And the prophecy is that only through the erosion of difference by great love and great suffering will the children of the Great Spirit find their common heart as they pursue their individual dreams. This is the paradoxical fate of all human beings: to release what is common and unsayable through the particular language of our heart that we try to listen to and voice.*

## A WORD CLUSTER

### Brahma

Sanskrit is one of the world's oldest languages. Its earliest appearance can be traced back to the Hymns of the Universe recorded in the *Rigveda* around 1500 BC. As original threads in the fabric of human language, words in Sanskrit are often more whole and all-encompassing than those in our descendant, modern languages. Frequently, there are no one-word synonyms for Sanskrit words as each often represents a more comprehensive way of seeing or being. Often, a Sanskrit word will point to a field of meaning, opening up an in-depth understanding of some aspect of life on Earth.

In English, the Sanskrit word *Brahma* is translated as the Hindu god who is the Creator but the word literally means "that from which everything arises, the Source of all." Brahma represents the unnamable, unending life-force that permeates all of life the way air fills the sky. In Hindu mythology, Brahma created himself in a golden embryo or universal womb and then created the Earth and all things in it. As such, Brahma is considered the force that created and still creates the Universe.

It is a telling sign of modernity that Brahma is somewhat lost to seekers today, seen as simply a pagan deity. This is another indication that we've been cut off from our direct connection with life and everything larger than us.

In the ancient Hindu texts *The Upanishads*, Brahma is

also viewed as the center of one's soul, which is our conduit to the Ultimate Reality, through which the Universe flows to awaken our being. How, then, can you open the heart of your inwardness so you can be rinsed into aliveness by the universal womb of all life?

## *A Question to Walk With*

Be present to three details that you encounter in your day until they start to show their connection to other life. In your journal, describe the three details and the spark of the Universe that your attention has revealed in each. Later, in conversation with a friend or loved one, share the three details you have encountered and the glimpse of the Universe you have felt in each. Discuss what this represents to you.

## A WORD CLUSTER

### Chung Yung

The legendary Chinese thinker Confucius said:

> *To find the central clue to our moral being which unites us to the Universal Order [Chung Yung], that indeed is the highest human attainment.*

It's interesting that in the Chinese expression for Universal Order, *Chung* means "central" and *Yung* means "constant." Thus, the highest human attainment is to find and sustain those elements within and without that are central and constant. The assumption is that uncovering and relating to these elements will link us with what has been central and constant in the Universe since the beginning of time. In spiritual, mental, and emotional ways, to live in rhythm with what's central and constant awakens an enduring sensitivity and strength. How, then, can you live in rhythm with what's central and constant, so it can be life-sustaining and foundational?

## *A Question to Walk With*

In your journal, describe one thing that has been central and constant for you during your life. What has it given you and taught you? How do you access it when you need it? Later, in conversation with a friend or loved one, share what is central and constant about your relationship and how it serves you both.

## A WORD CLUSTER

### haecceitas

The Buddhist word *haecceitas* means "this-ness, the ever fresh unfolding in the next moment." The this-ness or life-force waits like a shimmering atom in the center of each moment and following it is the balm of everyday life. Any task when fully entered leads us here. Inhabiting such elemental presence can also be elusive, because of our immense capacity to run from where we are and to complicate where we're going.

Awakening the conscious heart means entering the moment we're in while not being a prisoner of the past or the things we hope for. The gift of Now is to begin again with each moment; a task as simple and repeatable as breathing, if we didn't have to work through the tangle of our wounds and ideas. The challenge of Now is to feel all that has been imposed on us while knowing that these things no longer shape us. How, then, can you put down all that you carry so you can enter the this-ness, the ever fresh unfolding of the next moment?

## *A Question to Walk With*

In your journal, describe one imprint from what has happened to you that keeps you from living your life. How are you a prisoner of your past or your want for the future? Describe one step you can take to begin again freshly.

## A WORD CLUSTER

A-low-Haa
A-hoo-ee-Ho
O-ha'-na

These profound greetings are still in use in Hawaii today, where people live with the endless winds that seem to come from nowhere. Upon parting, one will say *A-low-Haa*, which means "may you always face the breath of Spirit," and the other will respond *A-hoo-ee-Ho*, which means "until our eyes touch." And finally, there's the Hawaiian affirmation *O-ha'-na*, which means "those who breathe together are family."

None of these greetings is incidental. Each reminds us that we are part of something larger and the remembrance of that kinship makes us family. For the breath of Spirit, like the wind, is everywhere though unseeable, feelable but not traceable. It is this wind of Spirit that moves from eye to eye, lifting us with some ancient connection that we have known and carried since the beginning. How, then, can you feel the breath of Spirit like wind, though it is unseeable?

### *A Question to Walk With*

In solitude, take a walk in silence until you feel the presence of everything larger than you. Note what has stirred this and what it touches within you. Later, in the presence of a friend or loved one, enact the Hawaiian greetings, voicing each with its meaning.

## Our Conversation Over Time

*The notions underlying the Hawaiian greetings, the Hindu concept of Brahma, and the Chinese expression for Universal Order reveal something central and constant about our walk in the world. Together, they point to a dynamic of relationship between the living part and the Living Whole.*

*The Hawaiian greetings remind us of all that is larger than us in which we are carried like a boat on the sea. The Hindu concept of Brahma reminds us of how the essence of the Universe lives within us like a seed or chromosome in the very core of our daily being. And the Chinese expression for Universal Order shows us how to connect that which is larger than us with the essence of life that lives within our core—by returning to what is central and constant in our living.*

*How, then, do we practice finding and returning to what is central and constant about life? All spiritual practice aims to make this question real. The Buddhist word haecceitas gives us a clue to how we might live into these dynamics—by awakening the conscious heart and surrendering to the ever fresh unfolding of each moment.*

*The qualities of life-force behind these words invite us to make personal vows of what they point to: to reconnect to everything larger than us, to listen to the essence of the Universe that lives within our core, to find and return to what is central and constant about life, and to awaken the heart by surrendering to the ever fresh unfolding of each moment before us. How might you personalize each of these vows?*

## A WORD CLUSTER

### tzu-jan

What makes life so challenging and exciting is that all this interplay—between the part and the Whole, between the individual and the Universe, between our time on Earth and the long, open trail of history—is unpredictable and ongoing. Life is always becoming.

In the Taoist tradition *tzu-jan* means "the constant unfolding of things." The word literally means "self-ablaze" and refers to the natural emergence of being through our unfettered heart-movements in the world. It describes the authentic, spontaneous expression that comes from living wholeheartedly in the open. When we are one with the life around us, our deeper self begins to blaze in the open, flickering like an unrehearsed flame.

This constant, unfolding rush of life is as steady and forceful as the ocean rising and falling on itself. Still, the tensions of survival get in the way and we often lose touch with this larger unfolding.

Only by being present and receptive can we find our place in the constant unfolding of things. This is the work of self-awareness: to position and ride our individual life in the river of days, as you would ride a canoe in the middle of a fast river. How, then, can you paddle your way with agility, humility, and grace?

## *A Question to Walk With*

In conversation with a friend or loved one, describe your journey through life as if you're riding a boat down a river. Describe the currents and turns you've had to face, how you've done so, and what you've learned.

## A WORD CLUSTER

### upaguru

Verse sixteen of the ancient Hindu scripture *Advayataraka Upanishad* reads:

> *The syllable gu means darkness, the syllable ru, he who dispels them.*
> *Because of the power to dispel darkness, the guru is thus named.*

And so, *guru* in Sanskrit means "mentor, guide, teacher, or master." A true teacher, then, is a guide who is committed to dispelling darkness.

Now, the Sanskrit word *Upanishad* means "a sitting, an instruction at the feet of a master." The word refers to holy texts written by Vedic poets between 700 and 300 BC. These ancient scriptures are thought of as instructions at the feet of *unseen* masters. As such, the Hindu *Upanishads* are considered teachings from the Mysteries of the Universe.

This brings us to the Hindi word *upaguru*. Since the prefix *upa* in Sanskrit means "near, with, or together," the Hindu word *upaguru* means "the teacher that is next to you in this moment." And so, my teachers include the wind, the stranger, and the broken bit of glass in the alley, the floating piece of conversation in the café, the light on the pigeon's beak as it pecks at bread crumbs, and the leaf stuck in the fence. For teachers are everywhere, ready to show us how to dispel darkness.

In truth, upaguru is one of my favorite words. It invokes a commitment to stay open and to keep learning. How, then, can you recognize the upaguru that is next to you as you read this? How, then, can you create a way of being in the world from how you meet and converse with the unseen masters of life?

## *A Question to Walk With*

In the next week, listen for the upagurus in your path. Journal about each, how they appear, and what they are teaching you. Later, in conversation with a friend or loved one, discuss each upaguru and the pattern of how they arrive and speak to you.

## Our Conversation Over Time

*In the Iroquois tradition, the god Taryenyawagon is known as the Holder of the Heavens. It's said that Taryenyawagon populated the Earth by sending clans of his people on a journey, each in a different direction, telling each to live and wait until they found their purpose. A direct calling never came other than to live as close to the land and water as possible. As each group grew more intimate with the particular land that held them, each developed a different language, the way the wind will make a different song as it moves through differently shaped trees. The lesson of this Iroquois story seems to be that a sense of purpose arrives from our particular commitment to living—as thoroughly as we can, where we are. This alone gives rise to the language of our life in all its magnificent detail. The lived-in detail of our lives holds open the door to the Heavens. What, then, is the sense of purpose that arises from the details of your life?*

## A WORD CLUSTER

nilchi
original
relic
ritual

The word *Dine*, which means "the people," is how the Navajo tribe chooses to name itself. The white name placed on this tribe, *Navajo*, was first used by Spanish missionaries in 1630. This name is derived from the word *nava hu* which means "place of large planted fields." Today, the Dine language of the American Southwest has only 150,000 speakers.

In the Native American worldview, the Dine word *nilchi* means "the holy wind that informs everything." This word describes the enlivening press of Oneness. This is yet another ancient term for the Spirit that emanates from everything. Unless we're in active relationship with the holy wind that informs everything, we live with the fragmented burden of believing that everything is chaotic and random.

Whether we acknowledge how everything is connected in the Universe or not, we're still impacted by its sweep and force. With this in mind, let's look at the word *original*, which doesn't mean to do something that has never been done before. *Original* means "going back to the origins." The word derives from the early sixteenth century French word *origine*, from the Latin *origo*, meaning "to rise." Therefore, *original* means to assume one of the many forms that rises from the Source. *Original* means returning to the holy wind that informs everything. To be original is to express, through the truth of our lives, the timeless holy wind as it moves through us.

In the early 1900s, the American poet Ezra Pound declared with fervor the misinstruction "Make it new!" In the hundred years since, artists and poets have become obsessed with being different more than being authentic and genuine. We've become more concerned with being unprecedented than being connected to the origins.

Consider Shakespeare, who wasn't original in the Poundian sense at all. His plays were all retellings of ancient histories and folktales. None of his plots were new. Yet what makes Shakespeare so remarkable and enduring is *how* he told these stories. For instance, Amleth was a Roman myth, but Shakespeare gave the story such psychological depth that he rendered the archetypal threshold of individuation that Hamlet faces like no one before or since. In doing so, he portrayed the indecisive pocket of heart that each of us carries.

The truth is that nothing is new. Rather, each expression of life is recurring and made new by our individual, authentic embrace. It turns out that our yearning to create is less about inventing something new as it is about inhabiting a timeless form, which might be new to us, through which we can feel the presence of all life in all time.

This brings us to the word *relic*, which means "that which remains, something worthy of reverence." A relic is some physical residue of reverence, a fragment of meaning that can remind us of what is original. A relic somehow has the imprint of the holy wind that informs everything. We hold on to relics not to worship a better time now gone but to remind us of all that is worthy and sacred in life.

Finally, we come to the word *ritual* which goes back to the Sanskrit *rta*, which means "visible order." So, ritual makes the order of the Universe visible. Ritual is a holy gesture or practice that brings forward the presence that informs everything.

All these forces are knit closely to each other: nilchi, original, relic, and ritual. For each brings what is sacred and ineffable into our presence. When open-hearted, we invoke the holy wind that informs everything. When original, we harken back to the origins. When we keep a holy fragment that has meaning in our journey, we invoke a relic of all that matters. And when we imbue a ritual of the simplest kind with our full presence, we are making the order of the Universe visible.

How, then, can you receive the holy wind that informs everything? How, then, can you be original, that is, be expressive of the origins? How, then, can you gather and honor relics that preserve meaning? And what rituals can you create that will help make the order of the Universe visible?

## *A Question to Walk With*

In the next week, invoke three personal expressions: (1) explore a creative activity by which you can experience the original nature of being alive; (2) identify a relic that represents a significant time in your life when you were in touch with all that matters; and (3) devote yourself to a simple ritual that will help make the deeper order of the Universe visible for you.

# The Journey to Oneness

*Though the things of this world seem separate, there's an underlying Oneness that connects all life. And while there's an ever-increasing language of delineation in the modern world that outlines and catalogues our differences, there's an enduring lexicon that reveals the Web of Kinship that joins all life. This chapter will explore that enduring lexicon. Through these words and their origins, we will examine how in unity there is diversity, how the particular, if held with reverence, always reveals the Common Center of All Life.*

*Inevitably, our journey to Oneness involves the reduction of the many into the One. Often, it's the relentless force of great love and great suffering that wears down our differences until we experience life in a way that is, at once, simple and profound.*

*However, if we only give allegiance to the language of difference, we will feel bereft in what life has to offer. For the language of dif-*

*ference is only life-giving inasmuch as it reveals the Oneness all difference comes from, the way all the various flowers grow out of the same earth, the way the 73,000 species of trees all experience the same necessity of growing roots and breaking ground. In just this way, there are a thousand paths between birth and death, though every soul must root itself in the enduring Oneness until it breaks ground in the particular life it has been given.*

## A WORD CLUSTER

adab

ahyo-oh'-oh-ni

In Sufism, the word *'ilm* means "seeking knowledge," and the purpose of knowledge centers on the notion of tawhid, the effort to affirm and access the Unity of God. In each person, this involves two sources of knowing: the outer knowing, *zāhir*, and the inner knowing, *bāṭin.* And the governing soul in each of us—that merges inner and outer knowing, that complements light with dark, that integrates our inner and outer experience—this is a person's *adab.* This word refers to one's place of inner steering. You could say our adab is similar to our true self.

One's adab is considered to be a living thing that we need to cultivate a relationship with. This speaks to an important difference between the ancient traditions and the modern sensibility, which views everything we encounter as instrumental to our success. Our adab—our governing, integrating soul—is not a screwdriver or a hammer. It's not some inanimate device we employ for leverage or an instrument we calibrate. Rather, it's a living thing with its own agency that we must work with and care for. In a similar way, the Spanish culture views courage as a living force like the wind that we don't conjure but must cooperate with.

When we can befriend the forces that move through us and around us, we have the chance to feel and join with the rest of life. The Native American Dine tribe calls this process of joining with life *ahyo-oh'-oh-ni*, which means "to bring one into harmony with everything." This is another name for our journey to Oneness. More than any outer success, this inner alignment with life is the deeper purpose of every awakened soul. More enduring than any achievement, this sense of harmony bestows us with the peace that comes from our deep immersion in the Web of Life.

## *A Question to Walk With*

In your journal, begin a conversation with your adab, the governing soul in you that integrates your inner and outer knowing. What do you want to ask your adab? How can you befriend your adab? Later, in conversation with a friend or loved one, discuss the challenges you are experiencing in letting your inner experience and outer experience inform each other.

## Our Conversation Over Time

*Just as I thought this book was coming to a close, my dear friend Rich ran across this word and sent it to me. I felt compelled to include it and best to place it here. The word is* tsundoku, *which is Japanese for "the stack(s) of books you've purchased but haven't read." The word combines tsunde-oku ("letting things pile up") and dokusho ("reading books"). First used in the nineteenth century, the word was a sarcastic jab at arrogant teachers who owned books but didn't read them. Today, the word more deeply implies that what we don't know is as important as what we do know.*

*In a more lasting way, being surrounded by all the books we haven't read is like going for a walk in the wilderness and standing among the ancient trees. You can feel the peace of the forest though you can't touch all the trees. In just this way, being surrounded by the books we haven't read is like standing in a wilderness of voices that feeds our soul. Or like rowing in the middle of a lake so you can drift among the countless waves that register the deep. We can never know the entire deep, though it carries us. Likewise, we can never read everything, though the depth of all that has been written carries us. To stand in the midst of all we don't know calms our nerves, breaks our self-reference, and entreats the world of Spirit to whisper in our ear.*

*I confess, I've always bought more books than I could possibly read. I'm simply drawn to the worlds they might open. I keep them near, knowing I will enter some at the right time, and that many will remain unread. Still, they surround me with their presence and web of connection. With this in mind, I encourage you to take some of the books you haven't read and place them before you. Simply place your hands on them and welcome all they offer, as you would the depths of the forest when you finally stop and place your hands on the trees within your reach.*

## A WORD CLUSTER

### alvar

In the South Indian Hindu tradition, the word *alvar* means "those who dive deep, those who are immersed." Ancient examples include the Twelve Alvars, the Tamil poet saints who remained immersed and devoted to the unseen masters who spoke to them through the Many Faces of the Universe. The trail of those conversations became their poems.

In particular, the Twelve Alvars were immersed in their devotion to Vishnu, the preserver and protector of the Universe, who returns to Earth in troubled times to restore a balance between good and evil. These twelve poet saints, who lived between the seventh and ninth centuries, retrieved and compiled four thousand Tamil verses that form the sacred *Divya Prabandham*.

In the daily life of the soul, we are ordinary descendants of the Twelve Alvars, each of us an honest breath away from being one who dives deep, from being one who is immersed. It is this immersion into the depth of life that awakens our soul and makes the connection between things knowable.

This immersion is our daily practice in being fully here. Being one who dives and one who is immersed is how we become a conduit for wakefulness. Being so fully present to the life within us and around us is how we take our place in the Web of Life. We could say that joy is the sensation of Oneness that comes from inhabiting our place in the Web of Life.

How, then, can you befriend your governing soul that is waiting to integrate your inner and outer knowing? How, then, can you commit to the journey of Oneness that will bring you a sense of harmony with other life? How can you learn to dive deep and immerse yourself as a way of life?

### *A Question to Walk With*

In your journal, explore one way you feel fragmented and separate from life. What might be the next step in your personal journey to Oneness? Later, in conversation with a friend or loved one, discuss what wholehearted immersion feels like for you and the last time you felt such an experience of depth.

## Our Conversation Over Time

*I have to bring Arthur into this book at this point. Arthur Zajonc is a world-renowned physicist whom I was blessed to work with for several years in my forties and fifties. He also believes in the common latticework of Spirit that words point to. By being true to how he sees and hears, he has his own all-embracing lens on the Living Universe that marries science and spirit. So when Arthur speaks, it's a song unlike any other. He has developed his own inner dialect, which is a natural outgrowth of where he stands as he looks out on life.*

*I love listening to Arthur speak. The way he weaves science and spirit is expansive and original, always opening doors I didn't know were there. He's a great model of how our expressive fields are natural manifestations of our inner experience. This is how language truly forms—as we live. Akin to how the warbler and the blackbird and the goldfinch uniquely grow their song. It's the honest conveyance of our experience of being alive that gives rise to our particular forms of speech. It's how I can close my eyes and hear your song and know it's you. Is there someone in your life whose language you are learning? Someone you love listening to? What is the intonation of your own inner dialect? Has it evolved through the years? How would you describe it? How would you name it? What is your deepest word?*

## A WORD CLUSTER

### manga

In contemporary Japanese, the word *manga* is used to represent the visual form of comics, cartoons, and graphic novels. However, the original word is composed of two kanji, the Japanese equivalent of Chinese ideograms, markings that convey concepts, images, or scenes rather than letters or words. The kanji that make up the word *manga* mean "impromptu or free-flowing pictures or drawings." The more comprehensive definition of manga is "the brush running away with itself." The masterful woodblock artist Hokusai created fifteen drawing manuals that are known as *Hokusai Manga*.

The notion of the brush running away with itself is at the heart of all creativity, the commitment to immerse ourselves enough that the work itself becomes our teacher and guide. This speaks to how jazz musicians listen for the music that wants to be played. It speaks deeply and directly to the sacred process by which I retrieve poems, stories, and metaphors: the need to devote our full being and attention to the nearest detail till it becomes a see-through moment. Until our woodblock, painting, melody, or poem becomes a picture of the floating world: revealing another seam to all that matters that waits between the particulars of being human and the vastness of life itself. Such moments write, paint, and play themselves. Such moments express, image, and release the melody that lives in us.

## *A Question to Walk With*

In your journal, describe a moment when you experienced the brush running away with itself, a time when your immersion and full attention allowed some particular of life to become your teacher and guide. What did such an effort teach you? What did such a moment open up to you and in you?

## Our Conversation Over Time

*The twenty-three Salishan languages are indigenous to the Pacific Northwest. The tribes of this First Nations people span from British Columbia in Canada across the American states of Washington, Oregon, Idaho, and Montana. The Salish languages are near extinction today, with some having as few as three or four living speakers and others, at most, about two thousand speakers.*

*In the Salishan language myth, two warriors hear a noise coming from ducks in flight and begin to argue whether the humming noise is coming from the air passing through their beaks or from the flapping of their wings. The argument escalates and can't be settled by the chief. So, a council is convened from the nearby villages. The council itself breaks down into more arguments. The longer the arguments go on, the more personal they become. Soon, the differences seem irreconcilable and ravines that seem uncrossable appear between families.*

*Finally, the hardened differences over what each has seen leads many families to uproot and disperse, settling far away from each other. Living in different places, the once unified people begin to speak differently. Once the people stop listening to each other, they become entrenched in their own way of seeing and thinking. Then, it's only a matter of time before they create different tongues and mythologies, insisting that their way of seeing and speaking is the most sacred.*

*This First Peoples creation story emphasizes the tension between the soul's call to Oneness and the human insistence on difference. This is a tension that challenges every one of us in our time on Earth.*

*For, eventually, we're all tempted to make a god of our opinion or a river of our questions.*

## A WORD CLUSTER

art
enthusiasm

The word *art* comes from the Latin *ars*, which means "craft or skill." But what kind of skill? If we look further, the word's Indo-European root means "to fit together." At the heart of it, we could say that all art involves the craft or skill of fitting things together. As such, it's a lifelong capacity that lives in everyone, for part of being human is the never-ending task of fitting things together. So, art is a creative, expressive means by which we come to understand the diversity of life on Earth.

The word *art* also shares a common root with such words as *arm*, *harmony*, *ordinary*, and *rite.* Such a confluence points to a perennial purpose of art: to discover and inhabit harmony through the ordinary ritual of making things. Whether we create a wheel, a garden, or a relationship, it's by fitting things together into a working whole that we make sense of being alive. The capacity of art that lives in everyone is a seed of transformation we each carry, a way of knowing and making that can lead us to what is true over what is great.

It's enlivening to create and fit things together. These efforts allow us to experience Oneness. Every time we work with what's before us, we're faced with the task of discovering, or *un*-covering, our *enthusiasm*, which means being at one with the energy of God or the Divine. The word itself comes from the Greek *en* ("one with") and *theos* ("the divine").

Despite our limitations, it seems that the qualities of attention, risk, and compassion allow us to be at one with the energy of the Whole and the *result* is enthusiasm. As such, enthusiasm is not a mood that can be willed or forced. Rather, it's the ripple that follows the stone once it enters the water. It can only be felt *after* we immerse ourselves in life.

### *A Question to Walk With*

In your journal, describe a time when you put things together to discover a better way. How did you discover that things needed to be put together? What new whole did they form? How did the process of putting things together affect you?

## Our Conversation Over Time

*We don't know who first imagined taking the feather of a bird and clipping its hollow shaft so that, dipping it in ink, you could write with it. We take it for granted now, but it was a mythic act: to fashion a remnant of flight in a way that it could convey words on a page. So that when the words would dry, someone in another time and place might read the words and be lifted in their mind or heart, as if they were being taken on an inner form of flight.*

*The best quill pens are made from goose, swan, or turkey feathers. Once the shaft of the feather is softened, the hollow tip is cut at an angle and the pointed tip is slit ever so slightly, so that ink will flow through the slit to the page. And the quill has a long history. There's evidence that parts of the Dead Sea Scrolls were penned with a quill. Later, legendary documents like the Magna Carta and the Declaration of Independence were also penned with oak gall ink through a quill. Even today, goose-quill pens are placed on each table of the US Supreme Court when it's in session.*

*The effort to tie a life of healing, peace, and rebirth with a life of flight is ancient. In Roman times, the windows of the sick were left open in hopes that the yellow bird, Caladrius, would flutter above their bed and take the sickness from them and fly away. And a Russian legend names the Alkonost as an enchanting bird with the head of a woman whose song would cause the most stubborn of souls to let go of all they've ever known, until they desire nothing for the rest of their lives. And perhaps the most mythic of birds is the Egyptian phoenix, an enduring creature that would catch fire in its own nest and, in time, a young phoenix would rise from its ashes.*

*For hundreds of years, we scratched out words with the feathers of birds, all in an unconscious effort to take away our sickness and to relieve our endless want, in hopes of awakening our souls in the face of pain and loss. So, find a feather if you can, a large one, and clip its shaft and scratch out your secret words with its inked tip and see if ancient birds will come to lighten your way.*

## A WORD CLUSTER

generosity
grace

Another way to experience Oneness is by being kind and generous. The word *generosity* comes from the Greek *plerosis*, meaning "a fullness that moves in all directions."

These continual ordinary efforts bring us into harmony with life itself: fitting things together, expressing and creating, and being kind and generous. In truth, being kind and generous is how we fit things together with love.

This leads us to the notion of grace, which traces back to an Indo-European root that means "in agreement" and "one who makes praises." Grace, then, is the moment of agreement when we're carried, however briefly, by the larger forces of life. Grace is when the part is in alignment with the Whole. It's not surprising that the word *grace* shares the same root as the word *grateful*.

Imagine a surfer who works hard to paddle out and wait for the next wave that will carry him. Eventually, in those brief moments when the surfer rides the wave, the wave and the surfer are one. This moment of Oneness is grace. But no wave lasts forever, and the surfer is thrust back into the water, waiting for the next wave.

Isn't this how life unfolds, with effort after effort trying to catch the next wave of grace? We can never tell when grace will appear, but we can paddle out and wait. The preparation that readies us for grace is a mix of art, enthusiasm, and generosity. This is how we find each other: through the enthusiasm that fitting things together releases in us, through the fullness in all directions that giving awakens in us, and through the Oneness that meeting grace with effort opens in us.

How, then, can you deepen these practices:

- fitting things together
- attending, risking, and caring
- being kind and generous
- and being in agreement with the currents of life?

## *A Question to Walk With*

In your journal, describe a moment of grace you experienced in which you felt a depth of agreement between you and the life around you. What led to this moment? How did it impact you? Later, in conversation with a friend or loved one, discuss your history of fitting things together. What are you being asked to fit together now?

## Our Conversation Over Time

*The French poet Paul Valéry said, "To see is to forget the name of the thing one sees." For all I've read, I had never come across this line. It stirred me. For to truly see is to look with our wholehearted presence until things appear in their original state before human beings began to pin names on everything. Such seeing returns us to the pulse of life that lives below all names.*

*I opened this book by recounting the moment during my cancer journey that I dropped below all names into the vibrant sense of life that exists below all labels and definitions. Ever since, a deep part of me has lived below all names. And this has been the well I return to in order to drink directly from life. This is where I retrieve the poems. Ironically, the only things worth writing about are those that can't be named or put into words. But we can point to them.*

*This is the true purpose of naming. For, as Paul Valéry affirms, a name serves as a threshold we can enter to experience the unnamed essence of a thing. And the reward for trying to name things is that such an effort opens us to a relationship with the thing being named.*

*However, all too often, in the habit of our thinking, we can accept the representation of the thing for the thing itself. We all know the shapes of the states that constitute America. We can draw any state on a napkin and easily recognize it. But when flying in a plane, those state lines are not there. We only see the unbroken continent in its oneness. Likewise, you may can fruit and shelve it in your basement. But the label is not the fruit. In truth, we often thwart ourselves when we mistake the map for the continent or the label of the container for the fruit the jar contains. We do this with love, heartbreak, and grief as well. In our fear, we use names to contain these emotions and put them on a shelf. Then, we store them in our basement and think that by handling the containers, we've digested what's in them.*

*Yet when we can live below all names, however briefly, we are returned to an Original Presence that sustains all life. This is how, as William Blake says, we can "see a world in a grain of sand." Or how the reach of one exhausted hand lifting someone who has fallen can hold the essence of all care. For when thoroughly present, one gesture of kindness can reveal the history of all kindness.*

*One of the things that poetry has taught me is that the aliveness that lives below all names waits for us to say yes to life. And saying yes to life lets us love ourselves and the world. These three presences are forever connected: what lives below all names, saying yes to life, and loving ourselves and the world. They lead us to our worth.*

## A WORD CLUSTER

holm
integrity
ma
mah
virtue

The British word *holm* (pronounced "home") refers to "a small island in the middle of a river or stream." Holm Island in England is a clear example. It sits in the middle of the Thames River on the reach above Penton Hook, near Staines, about twenty miles west of London.

Just what, then, are the small islands of sanctuary we can turn to in the relentless rush of days? What small havens in the middle of the stream keep us from being swept away? A few worth noting are the bedrock isle of *virtue*, the steadfast isle of *integrity*, the Japanese isle at the heart of the word *ma*, and the Jewish isle at the heart of the word *mah*.

It was the early Roman philosopher Plotinus who defined virtue as "our tendency to Unity." This is a more encompassing definition than the modern understanding of virtue as "behavior demonstrating high moral standards."

While our common understanding of virtue gives us a checklist of good behavior by which to maintain our sense of character, Plotinus suggests the aim of moral behavior is to become Whole more than good. He suggests that acting with authenticity and kindness will allow us to experience Unity and Oneness. So, practicing virtue has a deeper aim than being obedient and a greater reward than being approved of. The enduring reward of virtue is to inhabit Oneness, where we feel what it is to be a living part in a living Whole, and feel the strength that comes from such connection.

With this in mind, it's interesting that the word *integrity* means "to make whole." In spiritual terms, the work of integrity is the art of inner soundness that honors our virtue, our tendency to Unity. Integrity is the ongoing act of staying undivided in an effort to live life. This felt sense of integrity is our home, our island in the stream of time.

In late 2000, just months before 9/11, I was speaking at a conference at the World Trade Center in New York City. After my talk, I wandered into another room where Rabbi Jonathan Omer-Man was speaking about the life of integrity. I'll never forget his way of looking at this. He said, "Integrity is listening to the voice inside that doesn't change, though the life that carries it may change."

That voice inside that doesn't change, no matter how you name it, is our island in the stream, the deep residence of being that can withstand the endless changes we go through for being human. In the most profound way, integrity is the art of changing without changing. That is, embracing the changes as we go that let us maintain our foundational sense of being that never changes.

But how do we navigate between the inner place that doesn't change and the river of days that constantly changes? This brings us to the Japanese word *ma* which means "the space between." It refers to the consciousness we rest in when life seeps through all our walls to hold us.

The Japanese ideogram for *ma* combines the characters for "door" and "sun." Early renditions included "door" and "moon." These picture-words depict the sunlight or moonlight slipping through the crevice of a door. *Ma* refers to the space of vulnerability through which the larger forces of life enter the things of the world, including us. This space of vulnerability is yet another home or island in the middle of the stream.

Here is a simple example of ma. As I was working on this book in a café, a young woman against the wall was getting ready to leave. She had broken her foot and had crutches. She slipped her knapsack over her shoulder, balanced herself, then tried to carry an empty mug to the dish pan. She couldn't quite figure out how to use her crutches and carry the mug at the same time. This was when I saw her. I dropped everything and blurted out, "I can take that for you." Stunned that someone would help, she hesitated as I took the mug and dirty napkin from her hand. We both smiled as if to acknowledge, "Of course, four hands are better than two." And so, I entered the space of vulnerability that belongs to everyone, though we think of it as private. We had met on the small vulnerable island between us.

Rabbi David Ingber speaks about the Jewish notion of mah, which refers to the central question of existence and meaning. For *mah* in Hebrew means "what?" as in "what is this?" Rather than becoming entangled in "why" which is unanswerable, the Jewish tradition asks us to stay on the island of mah, where the question "what is this?" leads us ever more deeply into the living of life.

What is this eternal thing that keeps me going? What is the river of time I wake in that others have awakened in forever? What is this journey of suffering and pain and grief that breaks us open to each other? What is this thing that joins us at the most unexpected of times?

From the island of mah we can make our way, ever slowly and ever more deeply into the life of meaning, into the life of relationship, into the life of care.

So, where is your island in the middle of the stream? Where is the holm of your inner voice that doesn't change? Where is the vulnerable space between us where we can find each other? What is all this and how does it lead us further into our tendency to Unity?

## *A Question to Walk With*

In your journal, describe the island in the middle of the stream of life that you know as home. What sustenance do you find there? Later, in conversation with a friend or loved one, discuss the life of your integrity, that is, discuss the relationship between the voice inside you that doesn't change and the daily parts of you that do change as you work to stay real.

## Our Conversation Over Time

*With great delight, Leonard Cohen said that his grandfather could stick a pin through the Torah and know the meaning of every word it touched on the way through. This amazing image is a koan about the nature of learning. Just how did Leonard's grandfather come to such deep knowing? Did he know every word because of his lifelong study and contemplation of the lessons in the Torah? Or did he know every word because their meaning already lived in his heart?*

*The image opens us to two essential ways of learning: the effort of study and sustained attention, and the effort of intuition and the release of our innate knowing through experience. I think we must rely on both ways of learning. For each of us is called to study at certain times and to intuit at others. This is how effort works with grace.*

*What, then, is your history with these two fundamental ways of learning? Who has been a teacher and model for you in the way of study and sustained attention? And who has been a teacher and model for you in the way of intuition and innate knowing? How can the presence of your soul be a pin that releases meaning as it moves through the book of your days?*

## A WORD CLUSTER

### The Seat of Contemplation

citta
klong chen snying thig
kokoro
sentipensante
shantih
shing

The seat of contemplation is that all-embracing place below duality and complication where our deepest eyes look onto the world. Often, it's this underlying sight that marks the difference between our brokenness and our wholeness. Often, it's this heartfelt awareness that stirs the energy of love to rise out of pain. Often, it takes a feeling mind and a thoughtful heart to enter the realms of paradox in which the deepest lessons of life await.

In our modern tongue, we have lost the word for this integrated place. In fact, in our modern world, we often pit the mind and the heart against each other. Yet, in many traditions, the mind-heart is considered to be one perceptual organ.

In Japanese, there is just one word for heart and mind, *kokoro*. In fact, the Japanese ideogram for *mindfulness* depicts the heart and mind enfolded. It means "bringing heart and mind together in this moment."

The Chinese, as well, have only one word for mind and heart, *shing*. Similarly, the Chinese ideogram for *mindfulness* means "heart-mind-now." Elsewhere in the world, the fishermen of Colombia created the word *sentipensante*, which means "feeling-thinking," as a way to describe the place that can receive and speak truth.

Tibetan Buddhists also have a phrase for the deep-seated knowing that such feeling-thinking opens. It's known as *klong chen snying thig*, which means "the Heart Essence of the Great Expanse, the Mind-Treasure revealed." Akin to this is the Sanskrit word that T. S. Eliot made famous in his poem "The Wasteland," *shantih*, which also speaks to that place of deep-seated knowing. It means "deep peace that passeth all understanding."

And in the ancient Pali language of India, *citta* ("chitta") refers to "the mind-heart." Citta also indicates "a quality of motion, of fluctuation, a quivering" that characterizes how the mind-heart moves.

Still, we tend to study the ways of the mind and heart separately in order to understand their intricacies. We do this with many fields of knowledge. For example, in school, we study the geologic table to understand the elements of nature. However, these elements never appear so neatly or separately in the earth. In just this way, the dynamics of our mind and heart don't appear so neatly or separately in the terrain of actual living. In actual experience, the mind and heart are interdependent, inevitably cooperating with each other.

In true moments of living, the seat of contemplation is one of our deepest islands in the stream, the home of all our felt perception by which we keep transforming further into life.

How, then, can you practice bringing your heart and mind together in this moment? How can you listen to the feeling-thinking place that opens you to the sense of being that passes all understanding? How can these all-embracing moments unravel the fragments that tangle for living in the world?

## *A Question to Walk With*

In your journal, describe a moment when you felt your heart and mind working together. What did this feel like? Can you begin a conversation with that deep integrated place? Later, in conversation with a friend or loved one, discuss an all-embracing moment you have entered. What did this terrain look like and feel like and how did it nourish you?

# The Nature of Relationship

*We are constantly called to discern whether we will bring things together or pull things apart. So much of our journey depends on how we give and take. Two ancient myths bring these eternal choices into focus.*

*In Greek mythology, there is the story of how Hermes unwittingly betrays his divine calling. One day, Hermes, the swift herald of the gods, the revelatory conveyor of the Oneness of Life, brings diversity of speech to humanity. He feels certain that the Oneness of Life will only be revealed and strengthened if humans can find it from their own vantage points. He can't foresee that humans will misuse this diversity of speech to generate greater separation. He can't foresee that hiding in separation only leads to misunderstandings and a life of secrets. He can't foresee that individuals and nations will lose their grip on the Oneness of Life. In time, the various nations forget that such a Oneness exists. This leads the nations to become enemies.*

*This long devolution on Earth is but a few days in god-time. Over those dismal days, Zeus becomes so discouraged that he abdicates his throne as the ruler, protector, and father of all gods and humans. He feels all is lost, once humans have forgotten the Oneness.*

*In his absence, Phoroneus, whose name means "bringer of a price," becomes the first king of men. From that time on, Zeus imbues poetry and the arts with the forgotten language of Oneness. And secretly, Apollo—the god of poetry, music, art, oracles, medicine, sun, light, and knowledge—becomes his favorite. Ever since, the hope of restoring the forgotten language of Oneness has been the call of all poets, musicians, artists, healers, and teachers. How, then, can you be a student of the forgotten language of Oneness?*

*The second myth comes from India. In Hindu lore, Saraswati, the Hindu goddess of knowledge and art, was born out of the Saraswati River, the invisible river that carries the waters that sustain all life. Her name means "the one who flows." From the earliest times, the invisible river has sustained our natural resources as well as our human and spiritual resources, carrying actual water and the water we have come to know as truth and love.*

*Saraswati's ageless counterpart is the serpent-demon, Vritrasura, who is driven to hoard all the water on Earth. And so, the endless struggle is set: whether to be one who flows or one who hoards. In the* Rigveda, *the sacred collection of Sanskrit hymns (c. 1500 BC), the story unfolds that with help from her brother Ganesh, the provider and remover of obstacles, and Indra, the god who connects all things, Saraswati kills the demon who would hoard the Earth's water. And so, we are given a profound instruction. For it is eternally true that working our way through obstacles until we can connect all things helps move us from being one who hoards to being one who flows.*

*Those who would carry the water and those who would hoard the water keep appearing, again and again, within us and between us, so that we have chance after chance to learn this lesson well. Unspoken or not, aware of it or not, we take incarnation to earn our way back into the lineage of those who would carry the water, one more time. How, then, can you, in your daily practice, be one who flows and not one who hoards?*

*This chapter explores the physics of relationship and our need to be perpetual students of relationship in order to live fully. For it's the practice of relationship that allows us to enter the journey of inwardness enough to animate the nature of our soul. It's the practice of relationship that animates the nature of life as it comes through us. And the following chapters will explore the unending practices of relationship that allow us to devote ourselves to the commitments to living that will correct the missteps that keep us from living.*

## A WORD CLUSTER

academy
admire
akasha
chien

In ancient Greece, a young radical teacher by the name of Plato inherited a grove of olive trees near Colonus, about a mile north of Athens, where in 387 BC he began his school, the Academy, and convened informal gatherings. Plato had no particular doctrine to teach, but posed quandaries of living to enter and study together. From the outset, there was no distinction between the teacher and his students. They would simply walk through the olive grove together, trying to find meaning in their time on Earth. It's profound to realize that the original meaning of the word *academy* is "sacred grove."

In truth, there is a Sacred Grove waiting to be inhabited between us all. It is less a physical sanctuary and more a gathering place for those on the journey. True education depends on a covenant that all teachers make: to gather and walk through life's great questions with their students as companions. The holy space that comes alive when we truly behold each other and listen to each other has always been a source of transformation in the world.

So, one could ask: What do we do once we are in the Sacred Grove? This brings us to the practice of admiration. The word *admire* came into common usage in the late sixteenth century, from the Latin *admirari*, "to wonder at," "to look at with wonder." Just what does it mean "to look at with wonder"? What does it mean to admire someone or something? How does admiration work? What does it do to us to be admired? What does it do to us to be admiring?

The notion of *wonder* traces back to the Old English word *wundor*, which meant "marvelous thing, miracle, object of astonishment." When we admire someone or something, we lean into the power of life-force we find there so completely that we are astonished at the existent nature of whatever is before us. For to affirm what is steadfast and foundational, no matter where we find it, enlivens us.

Admiration is a powerful practice because when we admire someone or something, we are introduced to where those qualities live in us. Then, it is our work to stay in conversation with those qualities, to discern how to water them and nurture them. It is our work to let those qualities of admiration grow from within us out into the world.

The work of admiration leads us, again and again, into the Sacred Grove where life speaks and we listen, where we hold and are held, where we meet the harsh and soft circumstances of living while holding each other up.

When we can be this true and real with each other, the Sacred Grove extends beyond the place and time we are born into. Being so present opens us to the Sacred Grove that exists across the ages.

Carl Jung called this deep and open space across time the collective unconscious. In Sanskrit, the word *akasha* refers to a collective presence and memory among human beings. This collective presence allows us to recognize each other, though we've never met. It allows us to feel kinship with other souls across the centuries.

Whenever we open our heart and practice admiration, we become intimate with the life around us. And inhabiting intimacy is always a catalyst for the experience of Oneness. So, the Sacred Grove is any opening cleared by our authenticity to reveal the timeless life-force that enlivens all things.

In ancient Chinese mythology, the chien is a great symbol for our eternal connection with each other. The chien is an enormously colorful bird that has only one eye and one wing.

And it is believed that each chien has to find another in order to see and fly. In truth, each of us circles the sky of time like the mythic chien. Into this life we fall, needing to unite to fly.

## *A Question to Walk With*

In your journal, describe someone you admire. What is it you admire about them? And where do the seeds of these qualities live in you? Later, in conversation with a friend or loved one, discuss the Sacred Grove of your friendship. How do you walk with each other in order to explore what it means to be alive? What have you discovered together?

## Our Conversation Over Time

*At their deepest, words are windows which our full presence opens so we can be touched by the wind of being alive. Without opening them, words can only frame, reflect, and mirror. This is the difference between thinking and feeling, between conceptualizing and embodying. When conceptualizing, we peer through the closed window, which is fine, as long as we don't mistake what we see through a closed window as the experience of life with the window open. As Lao Tzu said, "Things may be named, but names are not the things."*

*Watching someone suffer is not the same as suffering yourself. And watching the river rush by is not the same as jumping into the river. Once opened, words help us live on the inside of things. Then, we are stopped in the middle of our schemes and dreams, stunned to be here at all. It is from this momentary opening of circumstance that we can bow our heads to drink from Eternity. Not to live there, no one can, but to be refreshed by all that never dies as we walk through the temporary world.*

## A WORD CLUSTER

common
The Commons
community
compassion
congenial

The eroded sense of the word *common* describes something so reduced by overuse that it becomes less than ordinary. This betrays the original sense of the word which is something so fundamental and lasting that it is shared by all.

The eroded sense of the word is captured in the phrase "the meaningless footfall of a common laborer," used to describe an anonymous slave working on the construction of the pyramids. While the original sense of the word is captured in the phrase "the depth of his pain led him into the common heartbeat that all humans feel," used to describe the central experience of living that all of us share.

It's interesting that the first definition of the word as a noun, the *commons*, refers to land that no one owns but which everyone benefits from and cares for. The simplest way to understand this is to imagine that you and I live on opposite sides of a lake. Our homes are personal and private, but the lake, which gives us water to live by, belongs to no one. The lake between us is the commons. It is in our common interest to care for the lake.

In the grasslands of Mongolia, shepherds maintain their individual homesteads but share and care for the vast grazing pastures, which stretch for miles between their homes and which are too big for any one person to own. Lobster fishermen in Maine maintain their small buoyed fisheries but share and care for the common waters. The air we breathe is yet another crucial commons, which everyone experiences privately but which no one person can own. While each of us needs to breathe, no one owns the sky.

Equally important are the resources that constitute our Community Commons, the covenants of relationship that hold a society together but which no one owns. And the Commons of Ideas, the web of foundational truths that bridge us and sustain us, which no one owns. And the Mystical Commons, the Unity of Life that we all depend on, like the water that fish swim in.

Which definition of *common* is affecting your life: being reduced to something less than ordinary by the anonymity of the modern world or the timeless center of living we all share? How can you renew your sense of wonder by caring for the Mystical Commons we all rely on but which no one owns?

The word *community* derives from the Latin "commun," also meaning "common." The same root informs the word *communicate* ("to have understanding in common") and *communion* ("to have experience in common"). And it's not by chance that the word *community* contains the word *unity.*

For community is an ever-potent seed waiting for our effort and care to animate what we have in common, so we can share our understanding and experience in our time on Earth. When truly in community, we can be more fully who we are by watering what we have in common. When in community, we can experience our common unity, which is always life-giving.

How, then, do we access the Common Unity that waits within us and between us? This is the purpose of *compassion*, which means "to suffer with, to become one with." At its deepest and most useful, compassion is more risky and enduring than sympathy or pity. For when compassionate, we agree to suffer with those we love. We agree to feel their pain and to alleviate the acuteness of their burdens. And being compassionate lets the Common Unity we all share flow between us.

Yet the Common Unity we all share isn't limited to the suffering that flows between us. It can join us, as well, through our common experience of wonder, joy, beauty, vulnerability, and moments of complete openness and honesty.

In its modern use, the word *congenial* means "pleasant or agreeable," but it comes from the Latin *com* ("with, together") and *genialis* ("kindred, of birth"). Its more original meaning, then, is "an agreement of being that we have known since birth."

So, when we can receive the part of a person that emanates

from the well of all Spirit, we find an agreement of being that we have known since birth. This marks the truly common experience of being alive, which is the bedrock of friendship.

Once we meet, listen, and help each other, we go below all the tangles of circumstance and discover our true kinship. For all the different paths of care lead us to the same Lake of Spirit. Drinking there reveals a bond we have known forever. And honoring our agreement of being alive enables us to endure and learn from our differences while renewing our common, more fundamental ways.

### *A Question to Walk With*

In your journal, describe an agreement of being that you share with another that you have known since birth. How might you name this agreement of being? What does it look like and feel like? Later, in conversation with a friend or loved one, describe a space or resource that feels like "a commons" to you; that is, it represents a resource that you and others need but which no one owns. What is your commitment to caring for this resource?

### Our Conversation Over Time

*Earlier, I explored two ways of knowing (through intuition and study) held in the image of Leonard Cohen's grandfather sticking a pin through the Torah and knowing the meaning of every word it touched on the way through.*

*Let me describe another mystical truth that is carried in how the words are inscribed in the Torah. In the Jewish tradition, the Torah is the compilation of the first five books of the Hebrew Bible and is often referred to as the Five Books of Moses. In Hebrew, the word* Torah *means "instruction, teaching, law."*

*Jewish lore holds that all the teachings found in the Torah were given to Moses by God on Mount Sinai after the Jews escaped slavery in Egypt circa 1300 BC. The complete Torah, as we know it, is believed to have been written on scrolls during the Persian Period, somewhere around 400 BC. In keeping with its origin, every Torah is written on scrolls by a holy scribe (a sofer). As the sacred center of the Jewish service, the Torah rests in an ark, a blessed alcove at the back of the altar, only brought out at the height of every service.*

*To uncover the mystical truth at the heart of the Torah, we need to look at how the Hebrew language is constructed. Derived from the Aramaic alphabet, the Hebrew alphabet has twenty-two letters. However, the vowels are not represented as letters, but as a series of accent marks and dots. In Hebrew, the positioning of the accent marks and dots reveals the pronunciation and meaning of various words.*

*This is significant because the Torah is inscribed without vowels, without any accent marks or dots. Why would the most holy text in this tradition be rendered without any guidance to its pronunciation and meaning? Students of the Kabbalah, the mystical tradition within the Jewish way of learning, claim that, as the most holy of texts, the Torah is void of any direct guidance to ensure that there can be no one, definitive meaning. For who among mortals has insight commensurate with God's vision?*

*Without the guidance of accent marks and dots, the Torah emanates many facets of meaning at once, no one more significant than another. And so, the meaning of the Torah is the mysterious sum of all interpretations. An early commentary in the Talmud describes the Torah as a mystical portal that has infinite faces and interpretations, making any singular definition of the Torah impossible. By its very nature, the reading of the Torah insists on the give-and-take of dialogue. It insists on a devoted form of listening to reveal the holy lessons residing there. This models an inclusive approach to life that challenges us to receive as many interpretations as possible, so that we can derive meaning from the true give-and-take of our lives.*

*I remember as a boy seeing the small wooden doors of the ark open at the back of the altar. The rabbi and the cantor would then lift the ancient scrolls together and place them on a podium before us. We would all stand and they would use a pointer to follow the mystical letters. They would recite the words, defying interpretation, and chant. I remember feeling a wave of sanctity drift over the room. It would settle into the spaces between our bones like an unnamed fragrance older than any of us. I remember leaving the service feeling somewhat renewed, though I couldn't put any of it into words.*

## A WORD CLUSTER

foreign
fellow
friendship

The word *foreign* traces back to the Latin words *foras*, which means "outside" and *fores*, which means "door." The notion of something or someone being foreign means they are kept outside the door. This sense of barrier has been quarreled with for centuries. Do we let others in or not? Do we demonize others as foreign to justify our reluctance to let them near? Whether in a family, club, neighborhood, or country, when do we stop seeing others as foreign and let them in?

Under all our rationalizations, calling something or someone foreign is a misguided way to say, "I have not yet bridged the distance necessary to know who you are or to become intimate with some aspect of life that is new to me." To conclude that something or someone is foreign is a self-centered way to say, "I am uncomfortable with you because you are different from me." Deeming other life foreign is like saying that what you see on the horizon is incapable of clarity when it is the distance that makes what you see blurry.

Ultimately, we are always called to get close enough to receive other life and so, no condition by itself is foreign. We are all challenged to open the door and move through the cloud of foreignness into the clarity of intimacy. Bridging this distance is at the heart of the human journey.

How, then, do we begin to bridge the distance between us that we mislabel as foreign? It often comes down to taking the risk to be who we are everywhere, which requires laying down our fears, defenses, and judgments.

This brings us to the word *fellow*, from the Old Norse meaning "partner, one who lays down wealth," which comes from the Middle English *welthe*, which originally meant "well-being." The fundamental notion of a fellow, then, is "one who lays down his well-being." Not laying down in the sense of giving up or relinquishing one's true nature, but rather in the sense of unfolding or opening the way between living things.

Ultimately, we are all searching—outwardly or inwardly—for the bridge of well-being, wherever we might find it. Why? Because in moments of being bridged we not only come alive, but, when in such accord with the Universe, we briefly become the Universe. So yes, I, too, am searching for the fellow—the other, the stranger, the conduit, living or not—who will serve as the bridge by which I might be joined to myself and thereby to the Whole of God's Being.

Creating and sustaining the bridge of well-being is the ongoing work of friendship. It is the never-ending practice of intimacy. The German root of the word *friendship* (*berg-frij*) means "place of high safety." The sacred grove of friendship goes by many names.

Tejas is the name of the Native American tribe native to the Dallas region of Texas. Tejas means "friendship." This is where the name Texas comes from, denoting "a land of friendship." The Japanese word for friend, *tomodachi*, is made of two ideograms. The first represents "two hands working together" and the second signifies "the effort to attain." So, the Japanese word for *friend* implies that working together to accomplish something creates friends.

The word for *friend* in Swahili is *rafiki*, which means "to be kind." In Swedish, *kamrat*. In Czech, *pritel*. In Hebrew, *chaver*. In Arabic, *sahib*, whose root is "truth." Thus, a friend is one who tells you the truth. In Latin, *amicus*; in Greek, *philos*; in Spanish, *amigo*; in Albanian, *mik*; in French, *ami*; in Italian, *amico*—all of which mean "to love."

We are ever challenged to dissipate the cloud of foreignness by laying down our well-being in order to be a bridge of love between living things. This leads us into the ongoing work of friendship, which is to sustain the bridge of well-being between all life, that place of high safety from which we drink of what matters and grow.

## *A Question to Walk With*

In your journal, describe something you consider to be foreign. Describe the distance between you and this piece of life. How can you bridge that distance and dissipate the foreignness? Later, in conversation with a friend or loved one, discuss the history of your friendship and what each of you had to both attend and give up in order to become intimate with each other.

## Our Conversation Over Time

*In 1817, the French pharmacist Joseph Bienaimé Caventou and the chemist Pierre Joseph Pelletier discovered the chemical present in all plants that we know as chlorophyll—the green pigment responsible for the absorption of light that triggers photosynthesis. Rather than name their discovery after themselves, they chose the name* chlorophyll *to honor the process they had witnessed in nature that was older than them. In their seminal paper, they wrote:*

> We have no right to name a substance [so] long-known, and to the story of which we have added only a few facts; however, we will propose, without granting it any importance, the name chlorophyll, from chloros, color, and φυλλον, leaf: a name that would indicate the role it plays in nature.

*These humble scientists exemplify the importance of true naming, which is to mirror the intrinsic processes of life over the self-reference that insists on letting others know that we were here.*

## A WORD CLUSTER

gacaca
priyankar

The Rwandan genocide occurred between April and July 1994. During these horrific hundred days, close to 662,000 members of the Tutsi minority were murdered by Hutu militias.

The atrocities were so widespread that when the rule of law was restored there weren't enough magistrates and courts in Rwanda to hear over 130,000 cases. And so, gacaca courts were instituted and hundreds of citizens were enlisted as official witnesses to hear the expressions of betrayal and sorrow in an unprecedented practice of Communal Listening.

In Rwandan, the word *gacaca* (ga'-cha-cha) means "being on the grass and listening to the stories of those who have been wounded." The painful need to be seen and heard proved, yet again, that bearing witness is a form of justice all by itself. For to listen to the stories of those who have been wounded is one of the oldest medicines on Earth. Bearing witness with an open heart is the seed from which healing and justice sprout.

Yet how can we do this for each other before the atrocities begin? One way is by practicing the Hindu art of a priyankar, which is Sanskrit for "one who must both do good for others and endure others." This ethic of goodwill rests on upholding our faith in our deeper capacities, believing in each other while holding each other accountable for our human frailties.

Isn't this the practice of staying in love? Aren't we asked to commit to believing in our better angels while enduring our flawed selves? Isn't love the daily practice of being truthful with each other while helping each other grow? Not judging or punishing each other for the gap but loving each other into closing the gap.

We need a sense of faithfulness that will stir the better versions of our selves. The social reformer Rudolf Steiner speaks of such faithfulness as the commitment to keep the true being of each other in view, no matter how briefly seen, especially when another acts in confused or hurtful ways:

> *You will experience moments—fleeting moments—with other persons. These human beings will appear to you then as if filled, irradiated, with the archetype of their Spirit.*
>
> *And then there may be—indeed, will be—other*

> *moments. Long periods of time, when human beings are darkened. But you will learn to say to yourself at such times, "I remember [their] archetype. I saw it once. No illusion, no deception shall rob me of it."*
>
> *Always struggle for the image that you saw. This struggle is faithfulness. Striving for faithfulness in this way, we shall be close to one another, as if endowed with the protective power of angels.*

How, then, can you deepen your practice of doing good for others while enduring their human frailties? How can we hold each other accountable while enlivening each other into surfacing our innate gifts? Loving each other while enduring each other is how our light informs our dark, how our strengths and flaws work together, how withstanding the gap between who we are and who we can be will allow us to know a grounded sense of love.

## *A Question to Walk With*

In your journal, tell the story of someone you believe in while enduring their human frailties. How do you understand their gifts and their flaws? How do you see them for who they are while sustaining your understanding of who they can be? Later, in conversation with a friend or loved one, discuss your own understanding of the gap between who you are and who you can be.

## Our Conversation Over Time

*A compelling paradox of connection is revealed by the early Christian mystics, the desert fathers of the third century, who gave us the metaphor of the Great Spoked Wheel. Imagine that each soul on Earth is a spoke in a Great Wheel and that no two spokes are the same. The rim of that Wheel is our living sense of community, and each spoke does its part to hold up the rim. But the common hub where all spokes join is the one Center where all souls come from.*

*As I become myself out in the world, I discover my unique gifts and find the one particular place on the rim of the Great Wheel that is mine to uphold. And so, as I move into the world, I live out my uniqueness. But when love and suffering cause me to go inward, I discover the common Center where we are all the same. When I dare to look into my core, I come upon the one common core where all lives meet. In our becoming, which grows outward, and our being, which grows inward, we live out the paradox of being both unique and the same.*

*The image of the Great Spoked Wheel shows us how we need each other. If any of these parts are removed, the wheel falls apart. Remove the rim, which is community, and humanity goes nowhere. Remove any of the spokes, which are the individual souls that make up life, and the wheel doesn't turn. Remove the Center, which is God, and there is no wheel. The practice offered here is to embody the paradox of our uniqueness and commonness by which the Great Wheel of Humanity turns.*

## A WORD CLUSTER

ningen
kuan yin
kalyana-mitta
interview
stranger
ren

The Japanese tradition defines the human endeavor as one of relationship. In Japanese, the ideogram for *human* (*ningen*), includes two characters: one for the animal we are, "the creature that walks on two legs," and one for "being in relationship." So, in the Japanese worldview, we, as humans, are understood as "the two-legged animal that walks in relationship."

The degree, then, to which we inhabit our humanity depends on the depth and life of our relationships, to everything: other humans, animals, nature, even the very air we breathe.

In the Buddhist tradition, the bodhisattva of compassion is *kuan yin*, also known as Avalokiteshvara. Her name means "hearing the cries of the world." This reveals that the key to all relationship is the art and practice of compassion and empathy by which we keep hearing the cries of the world.

In Pali, the language on which Sanskrit is based, *kalyana-mitta* means "spiritual friend." It literally translates as "water-drop-connection." This ancient notion suggests that relationship and compassion are the spiritual elements of friendship, equating the qualities of water—being clear, soft, and all-embracing—to the qualities of truly knowing the life of others in an intimate way.

As rain adds itself to the body of water it falls into, love moves like water through the cracks in the walls we build between us. And friends welcome a greater sense of life when they risk being with one another in a deeper way.

Of course, being human and living in the world, we stray and forget and have to find our way again, which we do by staying devoted to these enduring practices: true dialogue, finding the extraordinary in the ordinary, and following our benevolence.

It's interesting and uplifting that the word *interview* comes from the French *entrevue*, which means "the view between." And so, true dialogue is not one person questioning another, but both using their curiosity and honesty to still the turbulence of their days in order to see through to the bottom of things.

And while it is essential to maintain and repair the relationships we are in, we also must keep expanding our circle of relationship. This invokes the practice of bringing what is initially strange into our circle of empathy and intimacy. The word *strange* stirs us with a similar challenge as the word *foreign*, which I explored earlier.

The word *stranger* denotes "a living embodiment of that which is strange," and the word *strange* comes from the Old French *estrange*, which means "extraordinary." This may seem puzzling at first, but reflecting on it more deeply, the stranger can function as an unexpected messenger who can embody or mirror what is extraordinary within us, what is possible but not yet lived. The stranger, then, is an unexpected conveyor of growth, not harm—if we can bring what we consider strange closer.

The strange messenger, or the extraordinary completing agent unknown to us—whether it be a lover or a crisis—serves as a catalyst that opens us to a deeper way of living. Whether embodied in an event or in a person or in a break in our comfortable way of thinking, experiencing the extraordinary in the ordinary brings us closer to the Unity of Life in which we are all One.

In actuality, the strange messenger can show itself as anything: as a lyric of truth piped over our head in a restaurant, drifting into the center of our confusion at just the right instant; or as a sudden wind that relieves us of a certain map, forcing us to find our way by other means. Inevitably, the presence of such a messenger, whether arriving kindly or harshly, will reconnect us with the rest of life.

Eventually, we are asked to release our benevolence in a daily way. It was the Chinese philosopher Confucius (551–479 BC) who put forth that central to a healthy and enlivened social self is the core virtue known as *ren*, which means "benevolence, human kindness, what ties one to another." Ren is what holds community together.

In his *Analects*, Confucius tells us that ren depends on "trying to see things from other people's perspectives, and then to do one's best for them with that in mind." Confucius believed that every person is born with the capacity of ren within them, which manifests when a virtuous person treats others with humaneness.

Two hundred years later, Mencius (371–289 BC) writes that ren means "to be human, to be a person," and that "ren grows out of compassion, without which we would not be human."

Mencius gives this example. Ren is the spontaneous appearance of compassion that has us try to save a child playing near the edge of a well when we see that the child might fall in. It denotes our benevolence to others. Ren signifies that we are nothing when apart from our relationships.

As an ideogram, ren literally means "two-people-ness, co-humanity." Our moral life falls apart without ren. Without a relational self, our virtues scatter and we become a mix of jarring fragments. For example, we might be brave in battle but unkind at home, or ruthless in business but generous in church.

As Plato said, we are born whole but need each other to be complete. Like atoms, we are each distinct by ourselves but not alive till we join in relationship. And we come alive and stay alive by hearing the cries of the world, by being clear, soft, and all-embracing, by seeking the view between, by finding the extraordinary in the ordinary, and by following our benevolence.

Where are you in learning and practicing these skills of relationship?

## *A Question to Walk With*

In your journal, describe a recent moment in which you heard the cries of the world. How did this touch you? What did this teach you? What did such hearing move you to do? Later, in conversation with a friend or loved one, discuss your own history of following your benevolence.

## Our Conversation Over Time

*Some years ago, my oldest friend, Robert, and I experienced a sand-tray session together. Sand-tray work is a form of expressive therapy in which you place seemingly random objects in the sand of a tray to create a landscape that might convey an image of your unconscious mind. After creating a symbolic landscape, it's possible to interpret what that landscape is revealing about where you are in your life.*

*Whenever I've created a sand tray, it's proven uncanny, full of intimate meaning. Robert and I created our landscapes opposite each other and, after helping each other read the symbols tucked in the sand, we had the impulse to remove the objects one at a time in silence, until the only objects left were figurines that felt indispensable to who we are.*

*Robert's figurine was a sage-like man with a bird on his head, and mine was a horse running. Knowing each other so well, Robert smiled slowly and named me Horse Running. I laughed and named him Bird on Head. At the time, we weren't sure what these new and deeper names meant, but they felt absolutely true.*

*Now, after forty years of friendship, the spirit names we received that day have unfolded as attendant spirits. For in his essence, Robert is a quiet sage, so still at times a bird might land on his head and share its secrets of the sky. And I have always found what I know by running freshly like a horse into the light.*

*In modern times, we've drifted from the true purpose of naming, often labeling things to quiet our discomfort with uncertainty. But, again, we don't name things to pin them down or to keep them in place or even to have them bleed their meaning. We name things to be led by what can't be named.*

## A WORD CLUSTER

swanand sahayog sadhana
tarenga
ubuntu

It is a spiritual fact that we are more together than alone. It is this sort of honest acceptance of each other that makes true relationship possible. It is a sense of togetherness that Hindu sages call *swanand sahayog sadhana*, which means "the unfolding of blissful collaboration." Blissful because, once opened by our suffering, we understand in our bones that we are meant to join more than separate and that caring for each other somehow lets us blossom more completely in our uniqueness.

In inexplicable ways, giving of ourselves, paradoxically, allows us to grow. In Senegal, the word *tarenga* means "treating the other as the most important thing." It is a fundamental ethic of friendship. Somehow, when we treat the other as the most important thing, we mirror in our care our own possibility. In giving, we ignite our own gifts and unfold our blissful collaboration with each other and life.

In the *I Ching*, the ancient Chinese text of divination, hexagram 59 says, "When [our] hearts are won by friendliness, [we] are led to take all hardships upon [our]selves willingly." I don't think this hexagram is asking us to give ourselves away repeatedly. Rather, in this mysterious cooperation between hardship and giving, we are able to manage things together that we can't face alone.

By giving *of* ourselves honestly, we somehow become more ourselves and each other. By caring for each other, we reveal and hone our gifts. It's the life of authentic relationship that helps us endure hardship while letting us feel how precious the daily moments of living are.

The African notion of *ubuntu* is often translated as "I am because you are, you are because I am." It implies that we inevitably find our humanity in each other. Archbishop Desmond Tutu said that "ubuntu is the essence of being human: that my humanity is caught up in your humanity." And Dirk J. Louw, from the University of the North in South Africa, explains that "*ubuntu* is a Zulu word that serves as the spiritual foundation of African societies. It is a unifying vision that comes from the Zulu maxim *umuntu ngumuntu ngabantu*, which literally means "a person is a person through other persons."

The African ethic of ubuntu is founded on the irrevocable connectedness that exists between people. Based on this fundamental commitment to human kinship, there is no word for *orphan* in the African continent, because each tribe automatically assumes a lost child as part of its larger family.

At work here is the belief that in our very nature, we rely on each other to grow. As quarks combine to form protons and neutrons, which then form atoms, which then form molecules, individuals innately form families, which then form tribes, which then form nations.

Our strong need to interact stems from the irreducible nature of love. In fact, all the spiritual traditions are manifestations of our innate need to love and join. The practice that comes from the notion of ubuntu is the personal vow to water our common roots and to honor our strong need to love and join.

As Maria Popova says profoundly:

> *The capacity for love may be the crowning achievement of consciousness, which is itself the crowning achievement of the universe, which means that we may only be here to learn how to love.*

How, then, is the ethic of ubuntu working in your life? How is who you are made more visible and complete for your involvement with others? How does treating the other as the most important thing help you know your self better? How are you experiencing the unfolding of blissful collaboration in your days? How are you being honed into an instrument of love?

## *A Question to Walk With*

In your journal, tell the story of how caring for another revealed your own gifts to you. Later, in conversation with a friend or loved one, declare to each other that "I am because you are, you are because I am." Then, discuss what this means in your own particular history.

## Our Conversation Over Time

*My grandfather on my mother's side was a furrier in New York City. He was one of six sons who came from Romania. He and his brothers had dispersed around the globe: to Paris, Israel, Spain, Amsterdam, the United States, and Venezuela. When I was about nine or ten, my grandfather's elder brother Itzhak came for a visit from Caracas. It had been twenty-five years since they had seen each other. We all met in my grandfather's small brick home in Baldwin, New York.*

*I recall after dinner sitting in a corner of the small dining room. The kitchen was abuzz and other children were running around the house. My grandfather and his brother sat at opposite ends of the table, which still had empty plates scattered about. They looked long into each other, as if remembering when they were my age. Then, they started looking for a common language to speak. My grandfather knew six languages and Itzhak knew eight. I didn't know, at the time, exactly what they were doing. I looked puzzled and my father leaned closer and said, "They're trying to find a way to understand each other."*

*Later, I learned that they wanted to speak Yiddish, but Itzhak's*

*Yiddish was infiltrated with Spanish words and my grandfather's Yiddish was infiltrated with English words. After several tries, they settled on German and they were off, reminiscing and laughing. I sat somewhat aghast in the corner of that small dining room as their fluency filled the air. Now, I wonder about the kaleidoscope of tongues that make up the world and where life leads us against our will. And how, if we listen long enough, we find a way home.*

## A WORD CLUSTER

xenia
atithi devo bhava
hachnasat orchim

Despite the difficulties of living and because of them, our deepest and most reliable home is in each other's care. This has always been so. In ancient Greece, the term *xenia* held the ethic and custom of showing kindness to a stranger. The word means "guest-friendship." This was a form of hospitality shown to those far from home who happened by your door. Underlying this basic form of kindness is a deep trust in human nature, that without provocation we mean each other no harm.

In India, hospitality has always been based on the principle *atithi devo bhava*, which means "the guest is God." The assumption here is that the stranger bears a gift that can only be uncovered if loved into the open. And so, we are asked to welcome all guests as carriers of a holiness that once received will complete us. The implication is that the unexpected guest has what we need, if we will only welcome them. The same belief is found in the Jewish principle of hachnasat orchim, which means "welcome the guest."

Letting the weary traveler find food at our table and warmth at our fire makes everything less strange. More than a practice of occasional hospitality, these traditions represent a way of life, a vow: to offer friendship to wandering guests, to look for the divine in everyone who comes to our door, and to let weary travelers find warmth and food in our home.

When we can leave the door open to others, the world becomes smaller and warmer. This is the blessing of relationship, that the world becomes our home. The best of humanity has always shown itself when we let others in, only to discover that they somehow have exactly what we need, waiting in what they need.

How, then, can you let others in? How can you open the door of your heart and mind a little further? How can you welcome the unexpected wisdom of strangers into your home? How can you send others on their way, both of you illumined by your care and deep listening?

## *A Question to Walk With*

In your journal, tell the story of a time when someone welcomed you into the home of their heart and mind. How did this help you on your way? How can you offer such comfort to others on their way? Later, in conversation with a friend or loved one, discuss your own history of hospitality and how you have welcomed others during times of need and how this has affected your own growth. Who modeled such hospitality for you? Where did you learn to let others in?

# Commitments to Living

*Just what does it mean to commit to living? The word* commit *comes from the Middle English word* committen, *which means "to give in trust, to engage." This, in turn, traces back to the Latin* committere, *which means "to join together, to carry out, to release." So, to commit enlists the full gathering of our effort: giving our trust and our all in joining with other life as a means to persevere and release all that is life-giving. How we do this is quite personal.*

*The word* living *signifies "the condition of being alive" as well as the notion of "livelihood." Of course, the word* livelihood *has been appropriated by the press of existence to mean predominantly how we survive. But livelihood, on the inner plane, is more profoundly crucial to the condition of our soul. Once we can discern the conditions that are imperative to being fully alive, we can commit to ways of being, feeling, and thinking that can animate us as filaments of being.*

*While survival hinges on staying alive, our commitment to living depends on being fully alive. As important as all this is, no one quite knows how to do it. Yet each of us must uncover what it means to commit to living, so we can give our heart and mind to these sacred tasks.*

*To trust, to engage, to join, and release are all aspects of being fully alive. How, then, are you practicing these commitments and how are they deepening your condition of being alive?*

*With all this in mind, let me share the story of an enlightened, medieval king in Korea who improved the condition of being alive for his people. This is the story of Sejong, who found the courage to go beyond his own frame of reference in order to empower his people as they had never been empowered.*

*A Buddhist by nature and education, Sejong became king when his elder brothers, seeing his gifts, abdicated their chance to rule so that Sejong could ascend the throne. He quickly showed his innovation and compassion. For Sejong had an immense and gentle understanding of life.*

*This is remarkable considering the pernicious ambition of his father, Taejong. King Taejong was a crude monarch who murdered his own brother to gain the throne. To limit the possibility of rivals, he killed all four brothers of his queen. Surprisingly, Sejong assumed the throne while Taejong was still alive. What made Sejong's brothers abdicate their chance to rule? What did Taejong see in his son and why did he trust it, after a life of distrust? And what allowed Sejong to rule so differently? How did the compassionate son find and maintain his own identity under the cloud of a ruthless father?*

*The first thing Sejong did was to establish the Hall of Worthies (Jiphyeonjeon) at the palace: a gathering of scholars, sages, scientists, and physicians charged with furthering specific knowledge in science, medicine, and literature while making these advances available to all.*

*One of the first projects the Hall of Worthies undertook for Sejong was to create an agrarian handbook, to gather and preserve the experience of farmers. This effort became the first farmer's almanac. He also allowed his people to pay more or less taxes according to the fluctuations of their prosperity and hardship. When the palace had a surplus of food, Sejong distributed food to the peasants and farmers in need.*

*Even more remarkable was how Sejong, moved by the illiteracy of his people, instructed scholars in the Hall of Worthies to construct a phonetic language that would be easy to learn. Three years later, Sejong gifted the new language, Hangul, to the Korean people on October 9, 1446, through a royal document, the Hunminjeongeum, which means "the verbally right sounds meant to teach the people."*

*Within weeks, new practitioners, regardless of their background, were able to read, write, and converse. This extended literacy beyond the ruling class. With the creation of Hangul, knowledge and the conversation it opens became available to everyone. Now everyone had a voice. The gift of language removed the oldest wall between the villages of Korea, the thick wall of ignorance. As a life of exchange spread throughout the country, the culture became animated.*

*In his introduction to Hangul, Sejong wrote that he was saddened by his people's inability to state their concerns. And so, he charged the educated to help the uneducated, not just by sharing knowledge, but by offering the uneducated the means by which to become equal members of their society. He made literacy free and extended the capacity for voice to the Korean people forever. In modern Korea, October 9 is still celebrated as Hangul Day, honoring Sejong.*

*The story of a compassionate king who somehow came from a ruthless father is a powerful example that we are more than what is done to us. We are not doomed to the patterns we inherit. Sejong relied on a different kind of authority than his murderous father. Few of us will ever be kings or presidents or ministers of state, but to care about the concerns of those we live with, and to strengthen the web of connection between us—rather than tear it down—means we won't be alone in the storms or harvests that come.*

*This chapter explores the many ways we can engage and trust the conditions of living.*

## A WORD CLUSTER

acequia
admit
ahimsa

An acequia is a sluiceway or gravity chute that flows down a mountainside, providing water for a village. The Spanish word *acequia* (a-sā'kē-e), which means "ditch or canal," comes from the Arabic *al saqiya*, which means "water conduit." Late in the eighth century, the Islamic occupation of Spain brought this technique of irrigation to southern Europe.

When Spanish explorers came to the Americas, they found indigenous acequias already in use. In the Andes, northern Mexico, and the American Southwest, acequias exist as the outgrowth of ancient systems that carry snow runoff to villages and distant fields.

Many South American villages settled around the mouth of an acequia that begins high and out of sight in the crags of a mountain. There, the source-water collects all winter near the top and with the thaw it streams into the village. In Peru, entire villages climb their acequia each spring to clear rocks and tree limbs and animal nests, which during the winter block the path of water the village depends on. In Santa Fe, New Mexico, citizens annually clear a four-hundred-year-old acequia.

This is an essential metaphor for the flow between the Source of Life and the living. The metaphor calls for us to maintain our individual and relational practice of clearing out our acequia, a commitment to do so regularly, so nothing blocks our direct connection with the Source of Life.

Living by its very nature will cause our acequia, both internally and between us, to become blocked. What, then, are the practices and rituals by which you regularly clear the debris that comes between you and the Source of Life? How do you stay open and fluid?

There are many ways to address this. One is by being truthful to yourself and others. Like the villagers who live near an acequia, we need to stay clear and open by clearing our debris and letting life in. Both are conveyed by the word *admit*, which itself has two important meanings: "to say what is so" and "to let in." For instance, to admit the truth means, at once, that we declare things as they are and that we let truth in. It is the power of both meanings at once that helps bring our soul alive. It is the power of both declaration and welcome that constitutes the true art of confession.

One important aspect of meaningful confession is our unending need to admit who we are: both in admitting or declaring one's self, with all our gifts and limitations, and in admitting or letting in who we are. Both aspects prove essential and one makes the other possible. It is a strange but liberating dynamic of being: when we admit who we are (when we declare and own our gifts and flaws alike), we then admit who we are (we let in the deeper source of our aliveness).

Another way to clear our acequia is to return to harm-free living. In Sanskrit, the word *ahimsa* means "to cause no harm or injury." In its original context, ahimsa doesn't only mean the interruption of harm or injury, but also the commitment to live a non-harmful and giving life. Gandhi described the social meaning of ahimsa as "intercommunity harmony," affirming more what it is than defining it solely by what it is not, "non-violence."

The term *ahimsa* can be traced back in Hindu teachings to the *Chandogya Upanishad* (circa eighth to sixth century BC), where it is listed as one of the five ethical virtues. The Jain religion (ninth to seventh century BC) holds ahimsa as the first vow among the living.

Since all life-forms are deeply connected, what we do to others, we do to ourselves. This is an extension of the golden rule. The way of ahimsa acknowledges that harm begets harm and that the fire of harm can't be controlled. And so, who sets the fire is also set on fire. In the third century BC, southern India's Tamil poet, the weaver saint Thiruvalluvar, stated this truth as a spiritual law: "All suffering recoils on the wrongdoer himself. Therefore, those who desire not to suffer [must] refrain from causing others pain."

These ongoing commitments are essential to how we live. What is the acequia or path of flow between you and the Source of Life and how do you keep it clear and open? What is your practice of admitting, of saying what is so and of letting life in? And what is your practice of harm-free living?

### *A Question to Walk With*

In your journal, identify a form of debris that is blocking you from the Source of Life. How can you clear it? Later, in conversation with a friend or loved one, describe one way you need to admit to the truth of who you are and thereby admit or let in who you are.

## Our Conversation Over Time

*As a child, I received a library card as soon as I could sign my name. I was four or five at the time, and my brother and I drove my mother crazy, taking out what seemed like enormous books, forcing her to read to us while gazing in amazement at pictures larger than our heads. The sense of discovery was tremendous and caused me to realize, early on, that there was a world beyond me. Even before I could read, I tapped into the mystery of the written page, and books loomed as magical portals which drew me. I was never far from them.*

*I also grew up near the sea and my first true sense of solitude came when sitting in the bow of our boat, watching the endless waves re-*

*flect and go clear as they swelled and passed. My other lasting sense of solitude came in the presence of the books on my shelves. And now, it's hard to separate the two. For going where books take you, either in the writing or the reading, is so much like sailing out to sea. Being alone in our reflection is like being alone in the bow of a boat. In both instances, the world reflects in your face until suddenly, in a moment of clarity, you can see on through to the bottom of things.*

*Even now, there are stacks of books about my bed, which I open like willing friends, moving among them freely, reading and rereading passages that connect me to all that is essential. When I discovered I was a poet, the poetry shelves became a sanctuary where I heard soulful voices for the first time; a time-traveling oasis where I tried on many selves. As I grew in my own sense of consciousness, I found spirits there that understood, and frames of mind that made me feel less solitary. It was a secret camaraderie—steering my turbulent, adolescent heart through the honest currents of Rainer Maria Rilke, Hermann Hesse, Pablo Neruda, William Carlos Williams, Adrienne Rich, Robert Penn Warren, Muriel Rukeyser, Longinus, and Plato. I felt spacious in their presence and verified in a way of life I barely knew.*

## A WORD CLUSTER

appreciate
essay
faith

The word *appreciate* means "to move toward what is precious." Since everything is precious, making a vow to move toward what is precious is one of the simplest and strongest commitments we can make to living.

Obviously, things get in the way. When they do, it's imperative that we don't give up on the sanctity of what's before us but rather accept that our ability to receive that sanctity has been diminished. When the sky darkens and the clouds thicken, our experience of dampness and coldness is real, but it doesn't mean the sun has stopped shining. Just that we can't, for the moment, receive it.

To recover our appreciation of life requires holding nothing back and leaning into whatever is before us. How we do this is our personal application of care. And whatever slows you down, whatever causes you to remember the reverence of life, whatever softens and opens your heart is a practice of appreciation.

To keep moving toward what is precious, especially when things are in the way, calls on us to stay personal and specific. If I have a pebble in my shoe, it can prevent me from walking. The pebble is very personal and specific. I must stop, locate, and remove the pebble in order to continue with my life. Likewise, we accrue pebbles in the bottom of our heart and mind. And we must be very personal and specific to stop, locate, and remove those pebbles, too. So we can resume our life.

It's interesting that the word *essay* comes from the French *essai*, which means "attempt." It was the sixteenth-century writer Montaigne who first used the word *essay* as a way to describe an intimate form of writing he was exploring. Through his personal attempts to express and unravel the burden of his dreams, Montaigne invented the personal essay. Ever since, the personal essay has served as an instrument for honest inquiry into what it means to be alive.

In truth, whether we write it down or not, our honest and vulnerable personal attempts are necessary, if we are to remove the sharp pebbles of circumstance that get in our way. It is the quiet bravery of our personal attempts at living that allow us to return to a life of appreciation.

To move toward what is precious by holding nothing back, and to remove what gets in the way by the veracity of our personal attempts—these are commitments that inform our faith.

By faith, I don't mean belief in a doctrine or tradition. Rather, I define native faith as our commitment to the steadfast reservoir of being by which we know that life-force is ever near. By native faith, I mean the certainty by which we know that the sun is still shining beyond the storm that is wreaking havoc in our life.

The Protestant theologian Paul Tillich defined faith as "an act of ultimate concern." I hold this understanding of faith as crucial. For our wholehearted attempts to drink from life will result in acts of ultimate concern.

## *A Question to Walk With*

In your journal, describe the last time you moved toward something precious. What drew you there? How did this affect you? Later, in conversation with a friend or loved one, discuss the ups and downs of your ultimate concern. In specific terms, what can you attend that will deepen and strengthen your ultimate concern?

## Our Conversation Over Time

*Nehemiah was my father's father, the firstborn of a Jewish family that emigrated from Russia in the early 1900s. They landed in the Williamsburg part of Brooklyn. I barely knew my grandfather as he died when I was two. But everyone says I look like him. More deeply, he had a lasting love of books and language. I like to think that his stream of inquiry was reborn in me.*

*Later on, I learned that, before the Great Depression, Nehemiah worked as a printer for the* New York Telegram *in Manhattan. It was through this job that he learned English by arranging racks of letterpress type, a letter at a time. The story goes that he would quietly recite the words as he placed the inky letters in a row, moving his lips as he would repeat each word, over and over.*

*My father also had a love of books, though he was a slow reader. He built beautiful wooden shelves to hold stacks of worn books. These formed an altar wall of sorts in our small living room. I remember watching him on rainy evenings as he would take a book down and hover over it. He, too, moved his lips when he read. It was as if he were chanting softly under his breath.*

*I believe these generational efforts to learn helped to awaken the innate voice I was born with, the poet within who has led me around in my want to utter the hymns of the Universe wherever I can find them, moving my lips slowly and bowing to every letter of experience as each reveals a bit more of our common soul.*

*This might be the purpose of words: to have us discover what it means to be alive, an insight at a time. And to then recite our affirmations, over and over, until the words become oars that take us through the waters of time.*

## A WORD CLUSTER

immersion
devotion

How, then, do we embark on a life of appreciation, where authentic attempts lead us to a life of ultimate concern? This brings us to the original understanding of the words *immersion* and *devotion*.

The word *immerse* comes from the Latin meaning "to dip in." And the word *devote* comes from the Latin meaning "to uphold a vow." So while immersion invokes the giving of ourselves completely to an endeavor until it reveals its meaning, devotion asks that we uphold our commitment to stay immersed in that which has meaning until it becomes a way of life.

The sanctity at the heart of these words—*appreciate*, *essay*, *faith*, *immersion*, and *devotion*—constellate into a set of practices by which we can stay close to life itself. I invite you to personalize your relationship to each of these practices. Which come naturally to you? Which need more of your attention?

For me, the first step toward feeling what is precious involves giving my full attention to whatever is before me until it becomes my teacher. It could be dust on a windowsill or a loose feather stuck in the crack of a sidewalk. Or the breakdown of a stranger who confides to no one, though I happen to be near.

There are a thousand edges to what is living that can jump-start the heart, and a thousand turns of the journey that can jar the mind open. Any one can lead us to what is precious. Any one can stir us into an act of ultimate concern.

## *A Question to Walk With*

In your journal, describe a person, relationship, or process that you are devoted to. What led you to such devotion? How do you immerse yourself there and what does the experience of immersion feel like for you?

## Our Conversation Over Time

*Since the beginning of time, libraries and those who preserve knowledge and ways of knowing have created a lineage. The word* library *comes from the Latin* librarium, *meaning "chest for books," and from* liber, *meaning "the inner bark of trees." Implicit in the original sense of the word is the notion that libraries preserve the inner bark of humanity.*

*The first libraries date back to 3500 BC. They were composed, for the most part, of published records. Excavations from the ancient cities of Sumer, located in southern Iraq, revealed temple rooms full of clay tablets in cuneiform. At Nineveh, archaeologists discovered over thirty thousand clay tablets from the Library of Ashurbanipal, dating back to the eighth century BC.*

*Early Chinese libraries began with the Qin dynasty, where the library catalog was written on fine silk scrolls and stored in silk bags. Yet it wasn't until the eighth century AD that the Arab world began to import the craft of papermaking from China. One of the first paper mills was at work in Baghdad in 794. By the ninth century AD, public libraries started to appear in many Islamic cities.*

*In 983 in Shiraz, Adhud al-Dawlah created a magnificent library, described by the medieval historian al-Muqaddasi as "a complex of buildings surrounded by gardens with lakes and waterways. The buildings were topped with domes, and comprised an upper and lower story with a total of 360 rooms. In each department, catalogues were placed on a shelf and the rooms were furnished with carpets."*

*It was the hope of al-Dawlah to create a setting for his library that was a resplendent mirror for the fantastic worlds his books were windows to. From ancient clay tablets to entire libraries copied onto slim hard drives, the magic of books invites us into the history of humanity where the entirety of life is mirrored in a story or a poem or a personal attempt to make sense of being here.*

## A WORD CLUSTER

ichor
translate
ikigai

The long history of meditation practices helps us discover the bareness of being and the majesty of life just as it is. It makes sense that we need to slow down and still everything around us and within us in order to see and feel life in its glow. Once discovering that stillness, we often mistake the refuge of meditation as the only place we can find that bareness of being. Yet, I have discovered through the years that such stillness is the doorway to a bareness of being that is everywhere.

And one of the crucial commitments to living is to find and inhabit the majesty and glow of life out in the world through the smallest encounters with each other and nature. It seems we practice becoming intimate with life through practices such as meditation, only to bring that practice of heart-awareness into our days.

With this in mind, I want to affirm that our depth of living centers on three forms of elemental charge: receiving the spark of the Divine or life-force however it presents itself; receiving the spark of essence from one being to another; and receiving the spark of energy that comes from loving what you do. Let me say a few words about each form of spark by exploring the Greek word *ichor*, the Latin word *translate*, and Japanese word *ikigai.*

In Greek mythology, ichor is the ethereal fluid that is the blood of the gods and the immortals. It is what made them glow. In the modern world, ichor has evolved to mean "tenuous essence." This suggests that when fully alive, however briefly, we are infused with a trace of the essence of life that made the gods immortal. This signifies the essence of Spirit and life-force that has also been known as the spark of the Divine. For it is the spark of the Divine, however we come upon it, that causes us to glow. In those moments of being fully alive, we don't live forever but forever lives briefly in us. It enlivens us and blesses us with the wisdom of all time.

When we glow like this, we are experiencing what Abraham Maslow called "peak moments" in which the tenuous essence of the Universe moves through our open heart. Then, all our thoughts and feelings are informed by the history of all thought and all feeling. In such moments, there is nowhere to go, as we are filled with a sense of life that can only be inhabited, not achieved. To experience such an expanse of life is something we can only hope to encounter by meeting the world with a thoroughness of living and an openness of being. It is not something we can design or control or plan for.

The tenuous essence of life arrives like grace, changing everything while leaving no trace. But we can honor its power and presence and learn from how it touches us. And we can commit to a life of authenticity that readies us to experience such essence. How, then, can you ready yourself for the spark of the Divine? How can you become more thorough in your living and more open in your being? Ichor courses through your veins, as it did through the ancient gods, just waiting to glow, just waiting to be released by the thoroughness of your days. Let yourself be touched by all you encounter and life will fill us with its energy of essence.

The word *translate*, which comes from Latin, means "to carry or bring across." And the deeper vow of all poets and teachers is to bring themselves and others across the divides of ignorance and isolation into our kinship with all things. When we truly listen to each other, we help translate the truth of one person to another and to the world. When we truly receive another, we are carrying them from the confines of their solitude into a kinship with all life.

One of the great archetypal stories about translation and kinship is how Aaron would wait at the foot of the mountain for his brother Moses to come down from his audiences with God. Aaron would listen with excitement and insist that Moses tell the people what he had learned. But Moses, who had a stammer, told Aaron to speak on his behalf. And so, while Moses listened deeply to God, Aaron translated those divine messages to the people.

More deeply, Moses and Aaron represent the parts of us that commune with God and the world. We each have a direct, intimate relationship with the essence of life and we each have a translator who is called to bring what matters to others. How, then, do you care for these parts of you? How do you receive what lives beneath words and how do you give it through words to others? How do you translate your innermost experience to those around you? How do you carry your soul into the world? How do you tend to the life of your translator? For without the Aaron in us, we will live very lonely lives.

This leads us to the Japanese word *ikigai*, which can be translated as "a reason for being" which arises from matching our gifts and passions with the needs of the world. Once we discover the gifts we are born with by inhabiting our authentic self, the natural outgrowth of that knowing is to find where our gifts can be of use. The living of this natural movement from our inner life to our outer life gives us a sense of completeness and fulfillment that the poet Elizabeth Goldman describes as "a cup fitting in its saucer."

The symbol of ikigai is often represented by four overlapping circles which British community activist Marc Winn details as: what you love, what you're good at, what the world needs, and how this manifests as your profession. Where the four circles overlap in the center is the threshold of your reason for being, your ikigai.

For example, you might love helping things grow. There are many ways to do this. You could help people grow or plants grow or sea life grow or children. Once we know what we love, we can, in time, learn what we're good at. And so, through experience, I might discover that I'm terrible at being a farmer or a gardener but have some skill in listening and sharing or holding and mending. So, without veering from what we love, we might commit to helping people grow by becoming a teacher or a therapist, or to help people heal by becoming a nurse or doctor. When our inner gifts and outer applications align, we are on the verge of our reason for being, our ikigai.

A compelling metaphor for this is how a wooden match lights. We all know that the flame that releases light and warmth remains dormant in the phosphorous tip until that match is struck against a surface. In just this way, our gifts remain dormant within us until we strike them against the needs of the world. Then, we release our light and warmth freely.

Over time, our ikigai can change and evolve. For each giving of self and offering of service is an apprenticeship for the next. In unexpected ways, Albert Schweitzer's early work as an English teacher and a classical organist helped prepare him to become a doctor and to create his now famous hospital in Africa. And Gandhi's early work as a lawyer in South Africa helped prepare him to become the Great Soul who marched his people to the sea. We never know where we will test and hone our gifts, which may not be where we will ultimately offer them.

Yet, if we look more closely, there is an important distinction between how ikigai is understood in the East and the West. The notion in the West that what we love has to be tied to what we get paid for (our profession) precludes the joy in life that rises from our immersion and devotion. Tying our joy only to our profession confines our meaning in life to what is transactional, when the depth of joy, wherever it appears, is unconditional. The Japanese scholar Nicholas Kemp describes the threshold to our ikigai as "the value one finds in day-to-day living."

In a more daily way, then, ikigai can be understood as "the purpose that gets you out of bed in the morning." This beautiful ethic encourages us to stay devoted to what we love, whether that be a person, a calling, a craft or skill, or a way of life. For our love of life, however it shows up, has a magnetism that draws us out of bed and into the daily flow of places, people, and things.

The word *ikigai* is comprised of four symbols of which

*iki* means "that which arises from daily living" and *ga* means a shell like that of armor. The native sense of ikigai refers to that in our daily living that arises from putting down our armor and coming out of our shell.

So, if you don't know what you love, just open the shell of your heart and see what it moves toward. When open-hearted, we grow toward what matters, the way plants grow toward light. So, you can search and hunt for the key to your worth or you can open your heart and let life draw you out.

I encourage you to sit quietly in the center of your gifts until you begin to feel your ikigai, your reason for being. Not guessing what is needed and shaping yourself to it, but being who you are and giving it freely in all directions as light will naturally fill any hole.

I invite you to have a conversation with a friend or trusted loved one about what gets you out of bed in the morning. How does it appear? What does it say to you? What is it teaching you? And how is it shaping you?

Doing what you love can illuminate the jewel of your being. For every person is brought alive by a particular effort of immersion that lets the pearl inside your heart be the lamp of your soul. So, rather than prune yourself to fit how others see you, polish what you love and it will pull you into the day with vigor and excitement. Nothing is as enlivening or clarifying as giving yourself over to the act of loving.

If you practice whatever form of heart-awareness is before you, it will help you be more fully here. And I implore you to bring that heart-awareness out into the world. Open your heart to every hardship and blessing that's on your path. Welcome the bareness of being, through whatever spark it shows itself. Let life bring you alive with the blood of the gods that anonymously courses through your veins.

## *A Question to Walk With*

Take the time to meditate in silence and note a moment in which you touch upon the bareness of being that flows through all life. Journal about this moment. In the following week, be aware of where the feeling of life's flow might appear to you in the movements of your day. Journal about its appearance in the world. In another week, engage the Aaron-translator-voice in you and try to give voice to all this to a trusted friend or loved one.

## Our Conversation Over Time

*I was recently in Mexico, on the Pacific Ocean, where every morning dogs would run in and out of the surf until their human guardians would call them. I watched this easy ritual every morning. And thinking of my dog, I wondered how it is that dogs all over the world understand the language of the surf. Yet, at the same time, they understand the particular language of their people. The Mexican owners call for them in Spanish, while I call for my dog in English. How do they know the universal language of water and the specific language of those who care for them?*

*It made me think of the last time I was in Canada. I was walking the field beyond the retreat center where I was teaching, mull-*

*ing over a problem that was causing me some anxiety, when, like the Mexican dogs, I was drawn into the more universal language of nature. As I walked, I tried to work through my anxiety but the wind from behind a cloud brushed the thought of anxiety from my face and my worry entered a crow on the roof of a nearby barn. The crow started to caw. Then the dark bird coughed up my worry and began to fly. In that moment, I realized that we can't caw and fly at the same time. I never noticed this. Then, the wild grass was bowing to be coated by the light. And I thought, if I could only learn to bow.*

*Both in Mexico and in Canada, I was drawn into the language of dogs and crows as they pointed to the language of the ocean and the clouds. Like a pebble dropped in a lake, the language under all words ripples its way into the language of nature and on into the language of humans. One grows out of the next while the heart of all words offers its wordless pulse of life that is always near.*

## A WORD CLUSTER

Israel
journey

Between facing our own experience and perpetrating it on others, there is an ever-present choice that requires another kind of spiritual practice—one that wrestles to keep our inner and outer lives aligned and congruent. The ongoing struggle between these energies is, in some fundamental way, what we are put here for. Waking in the midst of these choices evokes an engaged practice of living that makes use of both being and doing. It is both receptive and active.

The Jewish tradition speaks of this ongoing engagement with experience as a necessary form of wrestling with God. The assumption under this sort of practice is that head-on engagement and heart-on engagement with the mysteries of life hone us to what is essential. It is a courageous engagement that wears away whatever is extraneous. Repeatedly, our vitality often comes alive when we wrestle with the energies of life.

This form of give-and-take is beautifully described in the Old Testament story of Jacob, when he "plunged down into the profound ravine of the Jabbok thousands of feet below." Reaching the strong river rushing at the bottom, he found the place of crossing. And there he waited, not sure for what, until an unnamed angel appeared and wrestled with him all through the night. At the sign of first light, the figure went to flee, but Jacob held on, saying, "I will not let thee go, except thou bless me."

Finally, the spirit gave Jacob its blessing and vanished as dawn flooded the length of the river. The spirit refused to name itself, but Jacob knew he'd seen the face of God. From that point on, Jacob was known as Israel, which is Hebrew for "God-Wrestler."

The essence of Jacob's journey awaits anyone who dares to search for God and who thinks truth might have something to do with it. And we are asked to understand this inner sense of wrestling, not as conquering or pinning God, but as staying in embrace long enough to be blessed by the unseen essence of life.

It is interesting that the word *journey* comes from the Old French *jornee*, which means "a day's travel, a day's work." It is still true that a meaningful journey is built on a day's travel and a day's work. We must wrestle and embrace the unnamed angel in all its disguises, day by day. This is how we become real and stay real. This is how we align with everything greater than us, so it can rejuvenate our Spirit.

### A *Question to Walk With*

In your journal, describe one way you are wrestling with the unnamed angel of life. What is it asking of you? What blessing do you want from it? How does this inform your day's travel, your day's work?

## Our Conversation Over Time

*The patterns of how we speak and listen to each other and how we record our histories say a great deal about the assumptions of a culture. The way our languages construct meaning evokes an implied education that we are seldom aware of. And so, we are often perpetuating inherited values without realizing it.*

*For example, the linguist Justin Smith-Ruiu reports that "In the Russian language there is no present-tense form of the verb 'to be' [and that] the Hopi language has nothing comparable to [the English] past tense." It isn't by accident, then, that an authoritarian society such as Russia, bent on suppressing the empowerment of the individual, would have no present-tense form of the verb "to be." And it is not by accident that an indigenous tradition such as the Hopi Nation, that keeps finding reverence in the ever-unfolding present, would have no form of past tense.*

*A more contemporary example comes from the Icelandic language, where there is no modern word for* computer. *The phrase that references a computer in Icelandic means "number prophetess." This naming implies that everything, even a computer, has its prophetic quality, emanating from a Mysterious Source that informs everything.*

*In contrast, the evolution of the English language reflects our modern preoccupation with our own agency and will. Relentlessly, the definitions and syntax found in English drive its users to assume that they are the creators of all they experience.*

*Earlier, I mentioned my book* Finding Inner Courage. *When writing that, I discovered that one way to ask "What does courage mean?" in Spanish is "Qué quiere decir el valor?" This literally translates as "What does courage want to say?" The difference inherent in the Spanish view is that whatever holds meaning is alive and has its own vital authority and, therefore, demands us to be in relationship with it in order to learn its meaning. The American view readies us to create meaning, while the Spanish view readies us to experience meaning as it already exists.*

*Even the rules of syntax in English betray our Western want to play God and be the sole arbiter of all we encounter. Consider our bias to the active voice over the passive voice. At one point in my book* The Endless Practice, *I talk about how a metaphor is seen, like a mountain we come upon. During the editing process, a well-*

*intentioned copyeditor corrected that sentence, wanting me to use the active voice, saying that we see the metaphor. But I believe we don't create the metaphor. Like courage, it exists outside of us and lives independently from our ability to see it.*

*So, I firmly intend the passive voice here, so that the world in which everything is alive can work its magic on us. In fact, calling this the "passive" voice doesn't accurately describe its qualities, just as the word* irrational *isn't the opposite of* rational; intuitive *is. I would rename the passive voice in English as the receptive voice. This allows for life to have its own agency beyond us. This begins to surface a syntax of being over a syntax of doing.*

*When we can think of language as a way to listen to the resources of life more than declaring our own agency, the definitions of words are more whole and all-encompassing. As best as we can tell, the earliest prehistoric names were words for rivers, as water has always been necessary to sustain life. And so, the earliest words convey concepts of what is larger than us, intoning notions of source and flow.*

*Historically, language is not limited to the words on a page. In Ghana, there is a percussive, drumming language used between villages, an auditory form of communication comparable to the Native American language of sending and receiving smoke signals across the skies between tribes. In the Canary Islands, the mountain dwellers of the fifteenth century communicated across vast canyons through a sophisticated language of whistling. And the Dine tribe of the American Southwest evolved a language over centuries of dance mixed with chants.*

*One of the most mystical forms of communication on Earth comes from the Aboriginal tribes in Australia, who have developed a language that deciphers songlines from their ancestors that are retrieved through dreams and conveyed through song cycles of dance, chant, ritual, and art. A songline is considered a timeless dream track that exists across the land and sky. We might call them seams in the fabric of Eternity connecting everything, always there but unseen.*

*The Aboriginal people believe that these essential connectors are briefly visible through the life of our dreams. Songlines have led tribes to discover waterholes. Once retrieved, songlines have led desert people to the ocean to engage in fishing practices. Through the tribal connection to songlines, it is believed that the ancestors deposit the spirits of unborn children into their just-birthed bodies. When a tribe faces a major decision, members travel the known songlines for guidance.*

*All this to ask: What inherited values are you upholding without being aware of it? And what innate language waits under all that has been imposed on your heart? What ways of speaking can empower your deepest sense of being, so you can sustain your direct connection to the Source of Life? And how can you keep waking into the ever-unfolding present? How can you stay in conversation with what courage has to say? And how can you stay true to your receptive voice? What will enable you to whistle across the canyon of your loneliness, so we might find each other? What language is that?*

## A WORD CLUSTER

Juyo Mukei Bunkazai Hojisha
lev tov

In 1955, after the devastation of World War II, the Japanese government authorized its Agency for Cultural Affairs to honor individuals or groups each year as Juyo Mukei Bunkazai Hojisha, which is Japanese for "Preservers of Important Intangible Cultural Properties."

Out of unthinkable harm a way has surfaced to nurture reverence and relationship. These preservers of the intangible are popularly known as *Ningen Kokuho*, which means "Living National Treasures." In essence, the award honors the recipient as a cultural ambassador, responsible for perpetuating the life of spirit and the life of community.

Ultimately, how we wrestle with and embrace life inwardly is inextricably linked to how we wrestle with and embrace each other. The life of the soul directly effects the life of the community. All this depends on the goodness of heart with which we meet whatever we encounter. In Hebrew, the words *lev tov* mean "good heart."

Committing to a day's work with a good heart keeps the Universe going. Committing to wrestle with and embrace the unnamed angel, however it appears, makes each of us a living treasure. In facing the abyss of self-interest and fear, we sorely need to preserve what is essential and intangible about life. This is how we participate in having a semblance of light dissipate a semblance of dark.

## *A Question to Walk With*

In your journal, describe one intangible property of life that you are committed to preserving. How do you experience this and how might you preserve this?

## Our Conversation Over Time

*When I think of the quiet power that resides in the fact that libraries exist at all, I'm reminded that one of the earliest librarians was a Babylonian named Amit Anu who was known as "Keeper of the Tablets" in the Royal Library at Ur nearly four thousand years ago. He was a scribe who was an elder.*

*Books are still necessary and everyone who preserves them and cares for them is a "Keeper of the Tablets," a descendant of this noble yet invisible profession of being guardians of what we know and how we know. Without such guardians, as William Butler Yeats has warned, "the center cannot hold."*

### A WORD CLUSTER

muhasiba
querencia
random

In the Sufi tradition, muhasiba is a practice of self-examination by which we're encouraged "to take an inventory of our actions, moods, behavior, and thoughts at the end of every day." This is not done to be self-praising or self-critical, but to develop an inner habit of course correction. For life is an endless series of aim and miss, of falling down and getting up, of try and try again.

How, then, can you take an inventory of your moods and movements in the world? By examining the impact your choices have on the life of your soul and the life of those around you. The key is to do so precisely but without judgment. For what is most important is that we course-correct, not linger in satisfaction or regret.

Akin to this is Yom Kippur, the holiest day of the Jewish year, the day of atonement, which can be seen as taking an annual inventory of the life of your soul and its impact on those you have encountered during the previous year. This is also done with the aim of course correction and an intention to make amends wherever necessary.

One fundamental aim of taking an inventory of our life is to return to the safe ground of well-being that holds us up in the world and to know that place as home.

The writer Georgia Heard tells us that

> *In Spanish,* querencia *describes a place where one feels safe, a place from which one's strength of character is drawn, a place where one feels at home. It comes from the verb* querer, *which means to desire, to want . . .* querer *means the wanting place . . . [So] what is your querencia?*

For me, the wanting place is not a place of surface wanting—for clothes or money or a car—but a place of relationship, a place of yearning in which I feel my want to return to the natural element in which my soul breathes. How do we find this place of relationship? How do we stay faithful to this place that feels like home, to which we return to heal? When was the last time you returned there? Do you still know the way?

As human beings, we are always moving between complete stillness and complete action. Both, entered wholeheartedly, open us to a thoroughness that makes us feel completely alive—one through ultimate being and the other through ultimate doing.

Consider a hummingbird when it hovers near a feeder full of nectar. Its tiny wings are moving so fast they don't seem to be moving at all. Perhaps this is the culmination of effort and grace, to be so thorough in any given moment of living that stillness and movement, being and doing, are one and the same.

To understand such thoroughness, we can look at the origin of the word *random*, which denotes the instant a horse has all four hooves off the ground.

The original meaning of the word refers to the mystery of unbridled passion, to the lift that results from total immersion and surrender. In our age, however, *random* has come to indicate chaos. It refers to utter chance, to events that unfold without design, method, or purpose. The trouble is that we often dismiss what we don't understand as random, thinking if we didn't author it, it must be accidental.

Yet our lives are full of unexpected surges that lift us which seem to come from nowhere. Just when you're thirsty, a cup is gathered and passed around. Just when you are lonely to the point of snapping that bone way inside that you show no one, someone offers you a ride or steadies the grocery bag about to drop from your grip. Just when you feel nothing can raise your sad head from the lonely road, several deer stutter across the road in exact rhythm with Handel.

So what might we learn from the horse at random? Consider how all of its energy and desire mounts for the brief moment it inhabits itself fully and, in that moment, it seems to fly. Only to touch down again. And to fly again. And touch down again.

For us, the moment at random is the moment of holding nothing back, of giving our all to whatever situation is before us. In that charged moment, we come as close to flying as human beings can—we soar briefly with a passion for life that brings all of who we are to meet our daily world. In that brief moment of full integrity, stillness and movement are one. Being and doing are one. Giving and receiving are one.

Our journey in life centers on finding our way back to this feeling of thoroughness we call home, to the wanting place of our heart, where we can rest in a lightness of being that is always near.

Reflecting on the nature of how we lift and touch down a hundred times a day led to this poem of mine:

THE WAY

*When a horse runs, it leaps*
*and touches down by turns.*

*In just this way, our life is always*
*moving between joy and sorrow.*

*Trying to avoid this is its own*
*sorrow, like a mad bird trying*
*to escape the sky.*

*Rather, our call is to help each*
*other rise and help each*
*other land.*

We are neither trapped on the ground, nor can we live in the sky. We must help each other navigate the rise and fall every day.

## A Question to Walk With

In your journal, take an inventory of your moods and movements in the world and describe three ways you need to course-correct. Later, in conversation with a friend or loved one, describe a moment of thoroughness you experienced that was, at once, completely still and completely at random. What led to this moment of fullness? How has it affected you?

## Our Conversation Over Time

*The legendary English poet John Milton wrote his elegy "Lycidas" as a memorial to Edward King, a friend of his at Cambridge who drowned in the Irish Sea when his ship went down off the coast of Wales in August 1637. In that poem, Milton uses the word* freak *as a verb for the very first time, when he refers, in a list of flowers, to "the pansy freak'd with jet." It's an amazing torque of meaning, in which the poet's grief recasts the noun* freak *into a bursting forth of color,* jet, *an archaic term for the word* black. *This is a small example of how the emotion behind a word can launch it into a new meaning.*

*It's worthy to note that John Milton was of the first generation of poets born after Shakespeare. Born in 1608 in London, he was a statesman, a diplomat, and an essayist. But his poetry was given no attention. Still, he remained faithful to his inner voice, no matter what transpired.*

*Due to untreated glaucoma, Milton's eyesight deteriorated until in 1652 at the age of forty-four, he went completely blind. This left him unmoored. But six years later, in 1658, depressed and impoverished, the blind poet, whom no one regarded as a poet, began dictating his epic poem* Paradise Lost *to a series of scribes, including his daughters. With no assurance that what he was doing was worthwhile, he stayed faithful to this inner voice that kept leading him.*

*It took six more years to complete his epic poem, which was published in 1667 by Samuel Simmons in an edition that contained ten books and over ten thousand lines of poetry. It sold for three shillings. And though he could hold it, he could never see or read a word of it. Milton showed us that when you can't see outwardly, you can see inwardly. He demonstrated how singular each soul's vision is, the worth of which no one can bestow or take away. In his sonnet "On His Blindness," written in 1655, Milton offered us his great instruction in the face of adversity, "They also serve who only stand and wait."*

## A WORD CLUSTER

rhapsody
saddha
serendipity

I chanced to learn that the Greek root of the word *rhapsody* means "stitch and sing." I found this stunning and thought, isn't this the art of being human, the ongoing act of stitching and singing? Isn't rhapsody how, when present enough and honest enough, we stitch ourselves back together? And doesn't the feeling of being stitched back together release our common song?

So, rhapsody is the weave between the pain of living and the song of living, not turning from one to the other, but making a tensile tapestry of them. With this in mind, we can experience George Gershwin's classic "Rhapsody in Blue" more deeply. Composed in 1924, it soars and dips and flutters with a fury of lift and enervation that spans all the human moods, as if taking the pulse of every neighborhood in New York City. It is, at once, tenderizing and uplifting.

In actuality, the act of rhapsody—of stitching and singing our way through life—is another testament to the mystical fact that all things are true.

This brings us to the Buddhist word for faith, *saddha*, which translates as "resting the heart in what is true." This is the recurring threshold to a life of authenticity. And the thoroughness we enter by stitching and singing our way through life allows us to rest our heart in what is true. In this way, the inner and outer journeys are forever knit together.

We tear and stitch. We heal and sing. Sometimes at the same time. We fall only to stumble into unexpected, serendipitous moments of wonder we can't foresee. In *The Professor and the Madman*, Simon Winchester conveys the origin of the word *serendipity*:

> *Ceylon, now Sri Lanka, was regarded by strict priests as the place to which Adam and Eve were exiled after their fall from grace, a place of evil and temptation . . . Arab traders called it* Serendib. *In the eighteenth century, [the English writer] Horace Walpole created a fanciful story about three princes who reigned there and who had the enchanting habit of stumbling across wonderful things by chance. Thus the English word* serendipity.

More deeply, serendipity refers to the moments of Eden here on Earth that we stumble into once we accept that there is nowhere to go other than here. There is no planning for these moments or seeking them out. But living a life of stitch and sing while resting our heart in what is true makes us permeable to such unexpected moments of tenderness and wonder.

## *A Question to Walk With*

In your journal, describe your current experience of stitching and singing. What are you stitching together? And what is the song that stitching has opened in your heart right now? Later, in conversation with a friend or loved one, discuss your struggle with resting your heart in what is true. What is calling you there? What is keeping you from going there?

## Our Conversation Over Time

*On November 12, 1857, a huge crowd assembled in the London Library for a meeting of the Philological Society at which Richard Chenevix Trench, the dean of Westminster Abbey, spoke. Trench explained why a comprehensive dictionary of the English language was needed and how it might be undertaken in a new way. This was the beginning of an immense community effort that eventually created the* Oxford English Dictionary, *engaging more than eight hundred enthusiastic volunteer readers and researchers, led by four editors over a seventy-year span. That night, Trench spoke in favor of describing how people actually use words rather than prescribing how people should use words. It was here that the basic principle of the* OED *was born: that use determines meaning.*

*This long moment of community devoted to advancing the availability of the English language to people all over the world would be a stunning accomplishment that, alone, might have reflected an enlightened culture. But in the same year, only seven months earlier, the same British nation, with ignorance and malice, had provoked the Indian Rebellion of 1857, in another case where use determines meaning.*

*The rebellion took place in Meerut, India, against the British East India Company. The insurgence arose because of what seemed a small thing to the British, whose engineers of war had devised a new breech-loading rifle, the Pattern 1853 Enfield. But the rifle had a fatal defect—not a mechanical fault, but a spiritual flaw. For the Enfield was designed to load a greased cartridge whose tip had to be bitten off before loading. And the British, indifferent to what they viewed as subordinate cultures, greased the cartridges with animal fat including beef and pork. In shipping boxes upon boxes of rifles and cartridges to India, it never occurred to them that many of the native Hindu and Muslim soldiers (Sepoys) enlisted at Meerut would refuse to put fat from a sacred animal to their lips.*

*So it was, on April 24, 1857, that eighty-five Sepoys in the Third Bengal Light Cavalry refused to touch the cartridges. After being court-martialed, they were sentenced to ten years in prison. By placing those Sepoys in irons, the ruling British triggered thousands of Hindus and Muslims to revolt. And though the British quelled that revolt, the sleeping giant of India had been awakened.*

*The 250 assembled in the London Library seven months later may not have thought much about the rebellion at Meerut or the brutality of the British soldiers who hanged thousands for sympathizing with the revolt. And if made aware, no doubt, many would have questioned what the* OED *and the Indian Rebellion had to do with each other. But we can question the values of a society in which so many were passionate about words but indifferent to the millions of Hindus and Muslims living then under British rule. For at the same time that Trench was speaking in London, the British Empire was flexing its muscle to maintain its harsh domination of India, which would drag on for another hundred years.*

*Holding the beginnings of the* OED *beside the rebellion at Meerut, I can't help but wonder: What if the reverence Trench invoked around the meaning of words had been invoked around the meaning of our lives? How are we to hold these two moments in London and Meerut in the same year in the same society? What are we to learn from them? If use determines meaning, how do we define honorable use? And how do we remember how to value people over things? For words are only holy when they bear witness to what is and remind us of what's possible.*

## A WORD CLUSTER

### the Sound One
### sumu

In Egyptian cosmology, the eye of the god Horus forms the sun. An early myth explains the sun's daily setting and rising as Horus's temporary loss and ultimate recovery of his central eye. The restored eye is known as the Sound One. Embedded in this myth is the endless process of loss and recovery. For the daily setting and rising of Horus represents our human cycle from blindness to sight, from turmoil to peace, our own recurring movement from darkness to light, as we spiral from confusion to clarity, again and again.

The myth of Horus implies that being *sound* is the state we find ourselves in on the other side of experience, seeing more clearly for having gone through life's encounters, not conquering or eliminating them. It implies that when fully alive and clear, we emanate light, and when closed off and out of reach, we wait in the dark.

In Japanese, the word *sumu* means both "to live" and "to be clear." This word affirms that to be clear is the lighted side of living. We can't, however, aspire to reside in this state of clearness and light forever. It is more ordinary and heroic that we outlast periods of turmoil, darkness, and confusion in order to restore our clarity and sight. This is our practice of return, as we endure the inevitable cycle of being human.

And so, both pessimism and idealism are great distractions from the work of being real. Even the Egyptian god Horus had to endure a temporary loss of sight repeatedly. It is pure hubris to think that we, as mere mortals, will never know dark. And pure defeatism to think that we will never know light. To be sound is to know both but not be intoxicated by either.

## *A Question to Walk With*

In your journal, describe the opening and closing of your central eye. Name one turmoil, darkness, or confusion that is currently keeping you from seeing clearly. Later, in conversation with a friend or loved one, discuss a return to clear seeing that you have experienced after a period of difficulty. What enabled you to return to being sound?

## Our Conversation Over Time

*One of the deeply binding qualities of friendship is how going through things together creates a common, inner vocabulary. Our shared experience yields a set of symbols that serves as a spiritual shorthand for the thresholds, patterns, pitfalls, and transformations we encounter. We discover our own personal reference points and, in larger circles, the literature of any culture begins to harvest a more widespread set of symbols.*

*"Dark night of the soul" is a powerful example of a term that represents the archetypal passage of spiritual development. St. John of the Cross, a medieval priest and mystic, is credited with coining this phrase in a poem of his that describes a pilgrim's inner journey to experience God. The phrase has come to signify a difficult and life-changing passage that ultimately leads to a new way of being. During the turbulence of being rearranged, things as we have known them no longer seem to work and our understanding of how to move in the world seems to go dark. Anything from the loss of a loved one to the shattering of a dream to the unraveling of our identity can precipitate a dark night of the soul.*

*The Jungian analyst Helen Luke adds to our spiritual vocabulary when she articulates the notion of a* quarter turn. *In her autobiography, Helen recounts a dream in which one of her oldest friends, now gone, is asked on the other side to weave a tapestry that tells the story of her life. But as Helen looks at the cloth, it makes no sense—until she gives the cloth a quarter turn and the pattern of her friend's life emerges plainly:*

> I suddenly knew I was looking at it from the wrong angle and I gave the cloth in my hand a quarter turn. Immediately I saw a beautiful and coherent golden pattern . . . In wonder, the pattern had emerged, to be seen in all its beauty by those who could learn to make the quarter turn.

*Helen then describes the quarter turn as a synonym for a paradigm shift, as a way to understand those unexpected shifts of perception that return us to the Hidden Wholeness that exists beneath all our assumptions and conclusions. And like the adjustment knob on a telescope or microscope that brings what we're looking at into focus, the quarter turn fine-tunes our perception, bringing into focus all that we see through the living instrument that is us.*

*We have all experienced shifts in how we see. It is not something to teach, but to lift up and share, to understand better, and to enter more fully. I experienced a profound quarter turn during my struggle with cancer. I was at one of many frightening ledges, needing to make another impossible decision. The tumor on my brain was pressing, and I had to say yes to surgery or chance waiting for further tests.*

*Then, on October 4, 1987, we had an early, heavy snow in the midst of autumn's full color. I woke that morning, tense and afraid of what lay ahead. When I looked into our yard, I saw that the early storm had brought all the trees down because the leaves, no matter how brilliant, had weighed the trees into snapping. If the leaves had let go, the snow would have left the trees standing.*

*This was a paradigm shift for me, which caused me to see holding on and letting go differently. I stopped trying to maneuver my way through my cancer and began to grow slim as a leafless tree.*

*Another personal example of a shared spiritual term comes from my lifelong conversation with my old, dear friend Robert. In acknowledging the constant interruptions and stumbles that come from tripping on the details of physical existence, Robert began to use the term* physica *to denote the endless grit of particulars that slow us down and sidetrack us. When the car breaks down, when the cell phone stops receiving calls, when the stone in your shoe makes you trip—these are the irritations of physica. The flux and jetsam of reality can slow us down and land us in confusion. In time, I offered the corresponding term* mystica *to denote the underlying terrain of Spirit that holds all of life together, despite the irritations and disruptions of reality.*

*All these terms are of great use in trying to assess where we are, what is happening, and where we might be going. Each of these phrases is shorthand for a deeply inevitable part of the human journey. And each of these terms is a personal way into all that is Universal. A single agreed-upon term can serve as a doorway to an entire process of life on Earth. No doubt you have your own. This is a deep and enduring power of words.*

*What, then, are some of the words or phrases that represent passages you've been through, and what constellation do they form of the deeper aspects of the journey you are on in your life?*

## A WORD CLUSTER

theater
vulnerable
veteran
war

The word *theater* comes from a Greek word meaning "the seeing place." It implies a fundamental law that we often resist: that wisdom is accessible only when we live out the truth of our experience. This embodied path is the seeing place from which we can know the secrets of being and living together. We can only go so far by conceptualizing or watching. Ultimately, we must live what we're given, singly and together, if the heart is to find and inhabit its place in relation to other life.

Discovering what's at the center of what we go through by living it out, by discussing it, and reflecting on it alleviates some of the burden we endure by carrying unprocessed experience.

Living from the seeing place allows us to stay vulnerable. It helps to understand that the word *vulnerable* comes from the Latin *vulnus*, which means "to carry a wound gracefully," to allow a wound to be filled with grace.

Physically, a wound must stay open to air and light in order to heal. If the wound is closed off, it can actually become more infected. So, to carry a wound gracefully is not to be closed off and stoic. Rather, it is to let light in so the wound can heal. This requires a quiet courage in staying open and vulnerable.

Often, this is difficult to do alone and so we need to return to the seeing place with the honest company of loved ones in order to process our healing.

I had a profound experience of this when I joined a psychodrama class offered by John Malecki, the wise, kind Jungian priest who led my cancer support group. The psychodrama group met monthly. Each session was centered on a dream, trauma, conflict, or wound that was burdening one of us. We first listened to the protagonist of the week tell their story. Then, that person would intuitively ask others in the group to take the role of different people and objects in the story or dream. Then, we would retell the troubling story by acting out the truth of the situation in real time with real people from the seeing place.

My first sharing with the group centered on a dear friend I had lost during those cancer days. Her name was Nur, Cheyenne for *light*. We were very close. When she died, she appeared to me repeatedly in dreams. In this particular dream, she was all aglow, even though her body was ravaged. She was thin and wore a bandana. She leaned in and asked me to join her on the other side. My heart was breaking. For I knew it wasn't my time to die. Yet she kept calling for me to follow her.

When we acted out the dream from the seeing place, the person I chose to play Nur stood before me as I began to cry, telling her, yet one more time, that I couldn't go with her, that she had to let go of me. At that moment, the person playing Nur looked at my hands gripping her, and asked, "Then why won't you let me go?"

I was shocked to see my own hands pulling her to me, while my voice was asking for her to let me be. This war in me between love and grief would have never been visible to me had we not acted out my dream. I couldn't work on loosening that knot until that moment because I wasn't aware it was a knot.

It's interesting that the word *war* traces back to the Indo-European root *wers*, which means "to confuse, mix up." War and the inevitable conflict it produces—both within us and between us—stem from a state of confusion.

Thus, a spiritual warrior is one devoted to the clearing of confusion, both inwardly and out in the world. The word *veteran* refers to "anyone having long experience or practice." It traces back to the Indo-European root *wet*, which means "to inspire or spiritually engage." The origins of these words confirm that our lifelong call is to carry our struggles while staying engaged, until we clear all confusion and re-establish our roots.

And the long experience of being here is to stay committed to the clearing of confusion and to carry our wounds gracefully, until we are veterans of life. This might be the most significant challenge of our times.

## *A Question to Walk With*

In your journal, describe a wound you are carrying gracefully. What does that look like and feel like? What can you do to embrace its healing? Later, in conversation with a friend or loved one, discuss how hidden you are with your experience and how you might process your experience more thoroughly in the seeing place.

# Correcting the Missteps That Keep Us from Living

*In the beginning, everyone spoke the same language. Thousands of years ago in the land of Uruk, in what is now Iraq, the early human family, still of one tribe, devoted themselves to building a single tower that would be taller than any structure ever built. Their hope was to create a visible landmark, so that anyone losing their way could simply turn and look to the tower and find their way home.*

*The entire tribe was united behind this purpose. But it took much longer than anyone imagined. By the time the third generation assumed the task, the tower, still incomplete, was so high that it took a worker almost a year to carry the next brick to its place.*

*But the grandchildren of the original builders really didn't carry the same devotion for the job. It felt more like a chore to them, having to build someone else's dream. Without their own devotion, it wasn't long before the press of the task consumed them. Finally, one day, a worker carrying the next brick fell, and they mourned the brick over the worker.*

*Of course, the broken landmark was the Tower of Babel, and shortly after this brick-carrier died, the now heartless workers, pressed to finish someone else's dream, decided to loot Heaven, upon which God confounded or confused their tongues. They instantly lost the ability to understand each other. The tower was never finished, and the human family, no longer able to understand one another, dispersed across the Earth, speaking different languages.*

*The medicine carried in this story tells us that the moment we value the brick over the person, we lose the ability to understand each other—we lose the privilege of a common language. And the moment we agree to build a dream we don't believe in, for whatever reason, we become enslaved to the task.*

*We each carry this possibility in us daily. But there is an antidote as well, carried in another story. It seems that generations after Babel, a mysterious spirit came to Earth, powerful in his gentleness and acceptance of human frailty. His ways were somehow threatening to the conquerors of the time and he was killed, but he had touched the lives of many in his short time on Earth. One of his closest followers felt compelled to keep his master's ways alive, but like the others, he was heartbroken and set adrift by his master's death. Confused and torn apart, he wandered for days. Then, Peter was stunned to meet Jesus again. He had come back to life. What this did to Peter was inexplicable.*

*Not long afterward, Peter found himself before a crowd of Jews assembled from all over the world. They spoke more than a dozen languages and there were no translators. But Peter could not be distracted by their differences, so strong was his need to share the profound experiences that had shaped and awakened him. Miraculously, as he spoke humbly and directly from his heart, everyone assembled understood him. They had been returned to the one original language that all beings share.*

*The medicine carried in this story tells us that the moment we dare to speak humbly and directly from our heart, we find each other. The moment we speak from the truth of compassion, we speak the same language always waiting underneath our differences. The mystery here is that when we speak from the Divine Center of Things, from our own understanding of God, things become one again. So we carry this in us, too: the possibility of Oneness.*

*These are the deeper, perennial valuations: how to know when we begin to value the brick over the person; when we begin to get lost in building someone else's dream; when we slip into speaking different tongues; and how to put the brick down, how to make the dream ours again, how to find the one tongue God has given us. We carry these possibilities within us every day.*

*This chapter explores the many ways we are challenged to refind the common language that is dormant between us, and how we can remember the enduring ways to value people over things, and how we can discern between the motivations that scatter us and the ones that bring us back together.*

## A WORD CLUSTER

alienation
ahamkara
mamamkara
absurd

This recurring danger of valuing the brick over the worker, which traces back to the Tower of Babel, is always a cold possibility whenever we are led astray from the sanctity of human connection. The dividedness or harmony of an individual often reflects or mirrors the dividedness or harmony of the society they live in. As early as 1844, Karl Marx told us that an estranged and divided society breeds an estranged and divided citizen.

He foresaw that when enough people are divorced from their basic human nature, this will give rise to an *alien nation*. From this understanding, Marx coined the term *alienation*. In fact, Marx thought of therapists as *alienists* whose primary commitment is to repair alienated individuals to their basic human nature.

The Industrial Revolution was burgeoning at this time. And with it, the center of work shifted from farm to factory. Home and work no longer happened in the same place. And with the fragmentation of division of labor, workers were no longer exposed to the full range of life's process.

For example, where a cobbler would make the entire shoe, most likely in a shop beneath where his family lived, a worker in a shoe factory would only make the heels of shoes, away from home. In time, this separation of work from living and the part from the whole divided people from their sense of self and their innate regard for others.

Marx believed that such alienation is a systematic result of unchecked capitalism, of people being treated like parts in a mechanized society. In deep and disturbing ways, our modern obsession with wealth epitomizes a society based on valuing the brick over the worker.

What's important here is to understand that we have to compensate for the estrangements that progress puts between us. For these estrangements still stand as impediments to the flow of kindness and compassion that originate in the universal regard that we are innately connected, that humanity is still of one tribe.

But this elemental choice whether to value things or people goes back even further to our dispositions at birth. In the ancient Indian language Pali, the word *ahamkara*, "I-ing," means having or making the feeling of "I," and it stems from the word *aham*, "I." The word *mamamkara* means "my-ing," having or making the feeling of "mine," and it stems from the word *mama*, "mine." In Buddhism, the feelings of I-ing and my-ing—of separation and possession—are considered so dangerous and poisonous that they are seen as the cause of "spiritual disease."

We can associate many modern ruptures of being with I-ing and my-ing. Often, the grip of these estrangements comes from seeing the world as only an extension of one's self, and from an insatiable want to have and own. Without undoing its knot, the pull of I-ing and my-ing can lead to a dark need to bring the world under our dominion.

This is ultimately unsatisfying, because the source of life's energies, though moving through us, exists beyond any one self. And trying to possess life, we end up hoarding and guarding life rather than living it. Painfully, the cycle of self-reference, if unbroken, unleashes a path of violation that corrupts our experience of being alive.

In truth, no one has ever lived without struggling between their sense of I-ing and my-ing and their sense of life beyond their small self. It is the trance of I-ing and my-ing that is toxic and debilitating. In order to break the trance of I-ing and my-ing, we must accept that our self doesn't author life but receives it.

In time, we are broken by great love and great suffering into accepting that no one owns what matters. We are simply blessed to be carriers of life while here.

With all this in mind, it's telling that the original sense of the word *absurd*, which comes from the Latin *absurdus*, means "deaf" or "out of tune."

And so, it is incumbent on each of us to discern when we are deaf to the Web of Kinship that joins us. We each must create a practice by which we can hear when we are out of tune with life and each other.

For without a return to our basic human nature, life seems absurd and meaningless. We each must personalize this ongoing remedy: how to put down the brick so we can care for each other.

## *A Question to Walk With*

In your journal, describe one way you feel separated from your basic human nature. What caused this rupture of being and how might you repair it? Later, in conversation with a friend or loved one, discuss the difference, as you experience it, between owning something and having something move through you.

## Our Conversation Over Time

*Imagine a weary soul who feels weighed down, exhausted, unsure what's next. He camps on a ridge near the sea and stares into the night sky. There, he sees a luminous constellation. To him, it looks like a weary soul with his arms draped on his knees, his head down. At least, this is what the silhouette of distant stars suggests. And so he names the constellation "the luminous drifter" and feels less alone.*

*At the same time, halfway around the world, a young woman stares out her night window through the cascading snow, where she sees the same constellation from another angle. To her, it is the image of a young woman, much like her, about to lift herself from the darkness that surrounds her, about to bloom, about to open her arms to Eternity. She names the constellation "the one about to waken," and feels less alone.*

*At the same time, on the edge of the desert, a wizened hunter tired of hunting squats in the night brush as he waits for the next gazelle. His gaze is drawn skyward like the others. Only he sees one of his ancestors there, squatting in anticipation of the hunt, waiting for the sun. He names the constellation "the hunt is in the wait," and feels less alone.*

*The stars remain unaware of all the names we give them. They emanate light in all directions whether we drift, wake, or hunt. The names we conjure from staring at the stars help us remember who we are and who we are becoming. They point us to a truth no word can contain.*

## A WORD CLUSTER

daimonion
anathema
analyze

In ancient philosophy, the word *daimonion* meant "the voice of the divine, the voice of conscience, a warning inner voice." In ancient Greek, *daimon* referred to a divinity or being of nature that exists between gods and humans; an inner, attending spirit or inspiring force. Socrates claimed to have lived his life according to the guidance of his daimon.

Originally, the notion of a daimonion included both guiding spirits and challenging ones. But somewhere between the Middle Ages and the Renaissance, daimonion was split into two words: *demon* and *angel*.

Ever since, the challenging spirit has been seen as evil and this false distinction has truncated our growth. This is a powerful example of a word eroding over time, and how its split parts are not as life-giving or instructive as its original whole. This break into two words has steered us away from what is challenging toward only what is comfortable and complacent.

The Native American tradition has preserved the notion of challenging spirits in the form of the trickster guide, an animal or elemental deity who leads us, often against our will, into the unfolding struggle of our transformation. It's important to understand that the trickster guide is not deceiving us but challenging us to think and act in ways outside of our patterned thinking.

Sadly, we, in the modern world, have cut ourselves off from any guidance outside of ourselves. And we suffer greatly for it. For there are teachers and resources everywhere, once we accept that we are inlets and not containers, once we accept that we are co-creators of life in an ever evolving Mystery that welcomes us but does not need us.

Psychotherapist Edward Tick, an expert on the trauma of veterans, reminds us that the word *anathema* comes from the Greek *ana thema*, meaning "against the theme of life, against the order of life, against the way of life." Tick says that all war is anathema, against the way of life, that such trespasses don't end when the physical violence is over. The war continues inside those who have chosen or been forced to take life. Yet, in our fear of what they've done and been through, we turn away from our veterans when they come home.

In a deep and internal way, daimons or attendant spirits, both comforting and challenging, help us return from all things anathema. They help us return from all things that sever us from the order of life. And, like veterans who have been damaged by war, the burden of our wounds can be relieved when we can receive each other and distribute the pains that living has rendered.

When we speak of daimons or attendant spirits, we are not just speaking of mythic angels and fairies, but the concentration of the unitive forces of life as they funnel through our individual lives, the way a lake feeds a stream. The concentration of these forces is known by many names: our inner voice, the voice of atman, the Holy Spirit, Adonai, the Great Spirit, the Sufi notion of the Beloved, and the voice of our soul.

Yet, how do we move in accord with the order of life? And how do we receive our attendant spirits? One way is by loosening the rigidity of our beliefs and by letting life in.

This brings us to the Greek root of the word *analyze*, which doesn't mean "to weigh and measure" but "to loosen." During the last two hundred years, our sense of perception has become ever more specialized; splitting, dissecting, and parsing whatever we find or create into minute parts. While such precision has jettisoned our progress, it has narrowed our sense of what life has to offer.

We sorely need to reclaim our ability to loosen our minds so we can apprehend and inhabit the Whole of Life. This loosening of the habits of our thinking will let us befriend challenging voices as well as encouraging ones. Broadening our outlook will let us befriend the order and theme of life. How, then, can you loosen your mind? How, then, can you loosen your heart?

## *A Question to Walk With*

In your journal, describe one way you need to loosen your mind. What is constricting you and what step can you take to get closer to the order and theme of life? Later, in conversation with a friend or loved one, discuss your history with challenging voices as they have appeared throughout your life.

## A WORD CLUSTER

### desahogarse

My dear friend David's daughter, Laura, is a psychologist whose clients are migrants who work the land around Santa Fe, New Mexico. Migrant work is hard and many, if not all of them, are without their families. They often carry a heavy burden, both externally and internally. And though they've experienced a great deal of what we could call trauma, they don't relate to that term or concept. Instead, she's heard many of her Spanish-speaking clients, mostly men from Mexico, use the word *desahogarse*, which means "to undrown oneself."

Pursuing what such a phrase means to them opens a compelling threshold for their sessions. Exploring how to undrown oneself feels more useful and hands-on than any concept of trauma. For exploring how we are drowning—emotionally, psychically, mentally, relationally—is the first step to unraveling trauma, especially in our modern world.

What moves me so deeply about the indigenous approach to life and its quandaries is that undoing a binding state, such as drowning, leads us to the tools that can resuscitate us inwardly. If we are drowning, what must we do to undrown ourselves?

Before I can repair things within me and around me, I need to understand how I break things within me and around me. Before I can solve my loneliness, I need to understand what it truly means to be alone. What changes if we begin to understand healing as the steps needed to undrown our lives?

### *A Question to Walk With*

Describe one way you feel like you're currently drowning. What would it mean to undrown yourself? Identify one specific step you can take to begin the undrowning of your life.

### Our Conversation Over Time

*In Irish mythology, Fenius was the learned king of Scythia who journeyed quickly to the site of the collapsed Tower of Babel with seventy-two scholars. It was his hope to talk with the fallen builders and to make some sense of what had happened. But when he and his caravan of scholars arrived, the fallen builders of the Tower had dispersed. So, Fenius sent his scholars after them, in all directions, to study their splintered forms of speech. After ten years, the king's scholars returned, bringing him the most meaningful expressions of each dispersed language, assembling them into the Gaelic language. From this, a Gaelic system of writing was created known as the Secret Language of the Poets. In the years that followed, Fenius distilled the common elements of the scattered languages, creating the other three major alphabets of Hebrew, Greek, and Latin. And through the ages, we have come to see that by extracting what is essential from all forms of speech, we can give voice to the Secret Language of the Earth.*

## A WORD CLUSTER

jihad
idiot
embarrassed
lost
todatsu

There are many ways we can stray from what is true and life-giving. We can be forced into a painful isolation by the pressures of a dispassionate society, or by a domineering family or partner, or by sinking into the depths of our own confusion which, unfaced, can become our personal demons. In fact, the original meaning of the Muslim word *jihad* is "to face one's own demons." Without facing what is ours to face, we can project the need to face ourselves until it becomes a crusade against others. This sort of distortion often leads to the cruel treatment of others and a self-isolation that severely diminishes our worth.

This enervating state of isolation was deftly understood by the Greeks. Consider that the origin of the word *idiot*, from the Greek *ídiotēs*, means "a citizen not involved with their community, a person who doesn't care about others." If we trace the word further back, we discover that the word *ídiós* refers to "a person collapsed into themselves." Being an idiot was a sorrowful condition, not a stupid one. It implies a walking state of disconnection and isolation, one which we suffer today en masse. And the road back to living with others in a meaningful way always begins with the work of facing our demons.

Often, we give ourselves away without realizing it, though when we recover our honesty and integrity, we realize there have been signs along the way. And when not able to be true, we falter into a weakened state of dissonance. At its deepest, embarrassment is a sign that we are dissonant, no longer congruent or true to who we really are.

The contemporary word *embarrassed* means "feeling awkward or ashamed." But the root word comes from the Spanish *embarazar*, which comes from the Portuguese *baraço*, which means "a halter," the bit placed in the mouth of a horse. And, in truth, not being authentic makes us susceptible to being led around by others.

Embarrassment, then, is a jarring signal that someone is putting a halter in our mouth, trying to lead us somewhere. Once we recognize that we are being led astray, we can realign our being and purpose. It seems an inner law: the more authentic and integral we are, the less we can be led around. And the less we are led around, the less harm we can do. It's important to note that we can lead ourselves around, too.

Often, the cure is hidden in the condition. It's more than coincidence that the Indo-European root of the word *lost* means "to divide or cut apart." And so, the inner meaning of being lost is to be divided or cut apart, no longer whole. When we are split, we are lost. When we are estranged, we are lost. When controlled by our demons, we are lost. When we collapse into ourselves, we are lost. And the only way out of being lost is to face our own demons in an effort to bathe our flaws in each other's spirit and care until we reconstitute the world.

To be led by our demons, to collapse into ourselves, to be led around by others or our patterns, and to feel divided and cut apart—these are all symptoms of being entangled.

This brings us to the Japanese word for emancipation, *to-datsu*, which means "a fish slipping out of the net." It implies that we must face and disentangle from everything that gets in the way if we are to transform. We are constantly challenged to slip out of the net, whether that net is imposed on us or of our own making. Having slipped out of several nets through the years and having woven even more, I'm drawn to understand our various forms of entanglement, and how our inner liberty depends on our ability to still ourselves, so we can slip out of the net.

Humbly, we're never done with this process, as no one can avoid being entangled. It's part of being alive. Yet whenever we slip out of the net we find ourselves in, we come alive like someone waking from amnesia. And so, our daily practice is to discern where we are entangled and how to still ourselves enough that we can slip back into the openness and depth of free living. Like it or not, getting entangled and becoming free form an unending rhythm that everyone has to apprentice in.

When feeling constrained, it is a reflex to push against what is holding us. But the secret to emancipation is to get small and still, so we can slip through the spaces in what is constraining us. Where are you, then, in your endless journey of slipping out of the net? What do you need to put down or let go of so you can free yourself? How can you sharpen your vision to better see the spaces in all that constrains you? How can you deepen your skill in getting small and still? How can you dive through the holes of light in the fabric of trouble?

There is always a chance of being caught in the nets of life, and there is always a chance to slip out of the net. It is the art of surviving until we thrive.

## *A Question to Walk With*

In your journal, describe one way you are being led around by others or your own patterns. Name one step you can take to stay true to your own voice. Later, in conversation with a friend or loved one, discuss your own struggle in facing your own demons.

## Our Conversation Over Time

*It is only through our humanity that we can fully access and inhabit the portion of Spirit we are born with. Yet, it is the flaws in our humanity that trip us up, time and again. One long-standing misperception about our life on Earth is how we've been taught to eliminate our flaws and, if we fail, to judge ourselves and others. But this is impossible. For there is no end to the depths and limits of being human. Interestingly, the Indo-European root of the word* human *means "to burn or warm." And being human, we are asked to continually burn what is false and warm what is true. We are asked to accept our humanness and correct our stumbles—aiming and missing and course-correcting as we go.*

*When we exile and judge our flaws, our rejected humanness will dominate our actions in the world. We will project our pain on loved ones, act out our insecurity on strangers, rage when hurt, and hide and mistrust what we can't find in ourselves. But when we can accept our stumbles and correct our ways of being, feeling, and thinking, then the life of our humanness becomes a conduit for Spirit in all directions. Then, we find what we feel in the company of others. Then, we are soothed for being tender and honest. Then, we can feel our kinship with everyone who ever lived.*

*Instead of cleaving pieces of our humanity to arrive at some imagined form of purity, we are called to enlarge our embrace of what it means to be alive—to include our humanity in all its expressions.*

*Our honest and compassionate acceptance of our humanity is the crucial difference between being tossed about in the surf of existence or being carried by the depth of Spirit that cradles everything.*

## A WORD CLUSTER

perfect
tamim
pleonexia
powaqqatsi
koyaanisqatsi
naqoyqatsi

In our modern culture, we have been steered away from wholeheartedness by gross misperceptions. This is made stunningly clear in a small compelling book called *Prayers of the Cosmos* by Neil Douglas-Klotz. He translates the words of Jesus into English from the original language he spoke, Aramaic, the native Middle Eastern tongue of his day.

In these original expressions, we discover, after all these years, that what we have translated as "be you perfect" (neth-qadash) really means "be you all-embracing." What we have translated as "Heaven" (d'bwashmaya) means "Universe," and what we have translated as "lead us not into temptation" (wela tablan l'nesyuna) is closer to "do not let surface things delude us . . . free us from what holds us back."

These mistranslations appear in other traditions as well. *Tamim* was an Old Testament Hebrew word meaning "wholehearted." But it was translated in the King James Version of the Bible as "perfect." These confining missteps narrow the path of what it means to be alive, resulting in a truncated frame of mind that impedes our growth in the modern age. For when we aim to be "wholehearted" and "all-embracing," we live one life. When we aim to be "perfect" and "unblemished," we live quite another.

These profound differences have skewed centuries of moral guidance. It seems we've taken a wrong turn! For the goal is not to purify the thousand things held to the light, but to drink them. It calls on us, not to live flawless lives, but thorough lives, not to seek perfection, but wholeheartedness. For to be perfect requires the elimination of our humanness, while to be wholehearted requires a thoroughness of living.

In the Aramaic language that Jesus spoke, the word *peshitta* means "simple, sincere, and true." The truth is that our flaws, when not hidden, are the simple, sincere, and true cracks that other life can fill, the way light fills a shadow or water fills a hole.

When we try to be perfect, we always fall short, which leaves us always feeling less than. This, in turn, leads us to always wanting more. In ancient Greece, *pleonektein*, from which we get the word *pleonexia*, referred to a condition in which a person lived with an insatiable appetite for more of everything. The Christian theologian William Barclay defined *pleonexia* as "a cursed love of having." Plato and Aristotle thought this condition to be the source of greed.

This insatiable appetite for more is a dangerous form of not listening that plagues the modern world. It speaks to our *fill-'er-up* society in which we think eating will keep us from the threshold of emptiness, and noise will keep us from the threshold of silence, and adventure will keep us from the threshold of being ordinary. When all the while, it's through the thresholds of emptiness, silence, and being ordinary that the true gifts of being alive wait to be discovered.

If we build a life on wanting more while avoiding emptiness, silence, and the blessing of being ordinary, we will be burdened with a life of dissonance and imbalance. Without facing our own demons and without being vulnerable and open to being touched by life, we spiral into a vortex of self-interest that can never be satiated.

Filmmaker Godfrey Reggio coined the term *powaqqatsi* from the Hopi tradition. The word refers to a way of life that bends or consumes the life-force of other beings in order to further itself. This describes the voracious appetite of narcissists to consume everything they meet in order to further their own existence. The Hopi-based term points to our unchecked self-centeredness, which continues to be a destructive underside of our humanity.

The term *powaqqatsi* combines two notions, *powaq* ("sorcerer") and *qatsi* ("life") and suggests a dark sorcery that twists life away from its aliveness. This is what happens when we stay addicted to the appetite for more.

Reggio created a landmark film trilogy based on these Hopi notions of imbalance. The first film is *Koyaanisqatsi* (1982) which is Hopi for "life out of balance." The second film is *Powaqqatsi* (1988). And the third film is *Naqoyqatsi* (2006) which is Hopi for "a life of killing each other."

All the traditions affirm that the only way back to our basic human nature is through the ancient and timeless medicines of holding and listening, through the courage to face our own demons, and the vulnerability that lets us receive each other in order to renew our place among the thousand living things.

How, then, can you curb your appetite for more? How can you befriend the eternal qualities of emptiness, silence, and the blessing of being ordinary? Where do these qualities appear in your daily life? And how can you renew your experience of holding and listening? How can you receive and be received?

### *A Question to Walk With*

In your journal, describe one way you experience the appetite for more and how it affects your life. Later, in conversation with a friend or loved one, discuss your own struggle between striving to be perfect and living wholeheartedly.

## Our Conversation Over Time

*Words can serve as warnings as well, symbolic of difficulty. Early on in my friendship with Robert, we were shopping in a grocery store when I spotted a whole catfish on a display of ice at the end of an aisle. If you have ever chanced to see a whole catfish, they are menacing and forbidding with a pugnacious snout surrounded by tentacle-like whiskers and piercing eyes. Without warning, they appear as a figure from Dante's hell.*

*Stunned by the unusual scene, I tugged Robert and said, "Look!" It jarred him and frightened him badly. Since that day, we refer to being jarred and surprised by any sudden experience that presents difficulty as being catfished. We have made a verb of the fish's name to signify this process.*

## A WORD CLUSTER

sabbath
sankofa
schizoid

In the Jewish tradition, thc word *sabbath* means "the one day we don't turn one thing into another." For instance, not turning stones into a wall or wood into beams. This fundamental request is at the heart of all rest: *to leave things as they are.* The assumption under the word holds the paradox that while we can build and create and better our condition, things are inherently fine as they are. It is a notion of life we can easily lose sight of.

Without a sense of life as complete unto itself, we depend on our list of achievements to give us our worth. Without access to the ground of being that rests under all our activity, we feel less than unless we stay busy. This push to do makes us anxious creatures who never leave anything alone. Then, we build in order to quiet our nerves rather than to better our condition.

But though we can forget what matters, we can also remember. The African concept of returning to wholeness comes from a word in the Akan language spoken in Ghana. The word is *sankofa*, which means, "We must go back and reclaim our past so we can move forward, so we can understand why and how we came to be who we are."

Words like *sankofa* encourage us to remember and reclaim the wholeness we all began with before the fragmentation of the modern world. This is not to romanticize earlier times. For being human, we have always struggled between being partial and whole. The struggle is just more acute in modern times because we are more isolated by the social conditions and technology of our age.

Throughout history, the estranged and partial state we find ourselves in has always been understood as toxic and unhealthy. In fact, the word *schizoid*, from the Polish word *schizotymik*, means "a person immersed and lost in themselves." An extreme and devastating version of this isolation is the condition of schizophrenia, the mental state in which an individual is so divorced from reality that they are imprisoned on the far side of a crack in the prism of life. Such out-of-balance isolation can leave a soul painfully adrift in a universe of jagged fragments.

The dark seeds of estrangement affect us all when we try to feed our anxiety rather than still it. So, the first step in regaining our wholeness is the quiet courage not to turn one thing into another, but to find and honor the innate state of soul we carry within. This will calm our agitation and help us be who we are.

How, then, are you faring in your struggle not to turn one thing into another? Are you building and achieving to buttress your sense of worth or to better our condition? Are you bouncing among the fragments of life or working to inhabit your birthright of wholeness? Are you feeding your anxiety or trying to still it?

## *A Question to Walk With*

In your journal, describe a time that you were lost in yourself. What did that look like and feel like? How did you find your way back to the rest of life? Later, in conversation with a friend or loved one, discuss how you might stop turning one thing into another and how you might drink more completely from what is.

## Our Conversation Over Time

*It was a brief, reflexive moment of nature, gone unnoticed near the beginning, a synapse of respect for other life. A small human, hunting on the side of a mountain, tripped and fell in a ditch as the herd of rams he was hunting came barreling toward him. Rather than crush him, the rams leapt over the fallen man. On his back in the ditch, he watched their white bellies glide over him. He heard the clomp of their hooves on stone as they sped away. And though a long history of men being cruel to whatever is in their way would follow, this inborn respect for other life is always near and possible, if we obey it. It waits in you and me, ready to leap out and help the world continue. Will you let it help the world continue or crush whatever is in your way? Will you honor life as you find it or be so lost in the difficulty of living that you trample the things you need before they can speak?*

## A WORD CLUSTER

science<br>conscience<br>thumos<br>upekkhā<br>tikkun olam

There is a long history of the gulf that exists between what we experience and what we internalize. Consider the words *science* and *conscience*. *Science* comes from the Latin *scientia*, "to know," while *conscience* comes from the Latin *consciens*, "to know well."

We could characterize the ability to know as retaining information and the ability to know things well as internalizing what matters. The impact of technology has extended dramatically what it is we know at a much faster rate than our ability to know things well. For to know things well requires time. But the advent of cell phones and microchips has thrust us into a life of incredible speed, where we are bombarded with much more than we can internalize.

The pace at which we know is exponential, while the pace at which we know things well is additive. And so, we can understand the difference between being constantly exposed to things and knowing things well as the cost of progress. The compelling question is how do we bridge the gap between information and wisdom, between knowledge and knowing, between a numbing catalogue of facts and the weave of insight and meaning, which can only be woven over time?

To navigate the cost of progress requires a fortitude of attention and care. It requires us to harness our strength and energy toward efforts of joining and building over efforts that deepen the gaps of separation and diminishment. The differences in how we use our strength and energy have a long history, too.

The philosopher Jacob Needleman speaks of the ancient Greek notion of *thumos*, which means "spirit of fight." The Greeks believed this to be part of our human nature. Whether it becomes a destructive or healing energy depends largely on whether that spirit of fight and struggle is directed in self-centered ways at the disappointments we experience in not getting what we want, or in deeper, transforming ways that work toward preserving the resources of spirit, love, and truth.

It seems to be persistently true that if that spirit of fight and struggle is not directed at diminishing what distances us from life, then it will be directed at others. Needleman suggests that the misdirection of *thumos*, our spirit of fight and struggle, has been a timeless source of war, evil, and unnecessary woundedness in the world.

How, then, do we enlist our energy to fight and struggle in our commitment to meaning over information, to joining over separating, and to slowing down over speeding up? How does this work in you personally?

This brings us to another perennial choice-point that we as humans face continually: the choice between self-centeredness and self-transformation. In Buddhism, *upekkhā* is a state of being that the Buddhist monk Bhikkhu Bodhi defines as the "freedom from all points of self-reference."

The flood of information and the bombardment of unprocessed experience can make us withdraw into ourselves, where everything about life is self-defined. This becomes an insidious and toxic way of being in the world because it eliminates all difference and diversity. Then, out of fear and reflex, we are confined to our own views and parameters. Until we are wrapped in a cocoon of self-reference.

Only the courage and strength to know things well can let other views in. Only listening with an open heart and an open mind can let us find our way into a state of being that is informed by all life. Once open to other life and other views, we can use our spirit of fight and struggle to repair the world and not break it.

The Jewish tradition offers the ethic *tikkun olam*, which is Hebrew for "You are here to repair the world." This instruction is at the heart of all transformation and service as discussed in the Talmud. We can trace the term *tikkun olam* back to the Hebrew phrase *mip'nei tikkun ha-olam*, which means "for the sake of repairing the world." This appears in the Mishnah, the first written collection of Jewish dialogues known as the Oral Torah, dating back to the third century BC.

In the high period of the Iberian Peninsula, during the twelfth century, the great Jewish rabbi, philosopher, and physician Maimonides understood the notion of tikkun olam as both inner work and outer kindness. In his commentaries, he wrote, "Through wisdom . . . and the elevation of character [represented by] acts of kindness . . . one continuously brings tikkun olam [into being, through] the improvement of the world and the ordering of reality."

In essence, this Jewish ethic suggests that the greatest work before us is to repair the world. And since we are the world, we have to repair ourselves first, the way a cloth is made whole when its threads are repaired. How, then, can you contribute to the unending work of transformation and service? How can you slow down and look beyond the confines of your self to the life of insight and meaning that reaches us through our ability to know things well?

## *A Question to Walk With*

In your journal, describe one aspect of your thinking or feeling that needs repair. How is it broken? How might you repair this? Later, in conversation with a friend or loved one, discuss your own experience of how the inner work of transformation and the outer work of service inform each other.

# Meeting Difficulty and Change

*This chapter explores the constellation of words across traditions that help us meet difficulty and change, that remind us that we're not alone when struggling, that offer us time-tried resources that we often forget are there. Often, in the sudden challenge of meeting difficulty and change, the strength and resilience needed are very close to the difficulty we have stumbled on.*

*Let's begin with the story of Sequoyah, a Native American who could neither read nor write who, in 1809 at the age of thirty-nine, began to create a written language for the Cherokee Nation. Twelve years later, he completed what is known as a syllabary, a written language comprised of eighty-six symbols that represent syllables in place of an alphabet. Remarkably, this quiet and gifted man, born of a Cherokee mother and a white father, created a language for his people, which is still used today, primarily in Oklahoma, North Carolina, and Arkansas.*

*No one knows what stirred Sequoyah to devote himself to such a task. But as a young man, he witnessed US soldiers reading script from paper repeatedly. He called the written pages* talking leaves. *From that point on, he became obsessed with creating a system of* talking leaves *for his people. He did so at the expense of his crops and his family. Hardship was a familiar companion to Sequoyah. From an early age, he was disabled, partially crippled by a knee affected by hydrarthrosis, commonly known as white swelling. Yet despite a lack of schooling, he became an accomplished jeweler and silversmith.*

*In 1815, he married a biracial Cherokee, Sally Benge, and they had a daughter, Ayoka. It was with the help of six-year-old Ayoka that Sequoyah convinced other Cherokees that his language wasn't a hoax or witchcraft. He would send his daughter into another room and ask one of the tribe to whisper a word to him. Then, he would write the word down in his new language and send the piece of paper to his daughter in the next room. She would accurately speak the word and everyone was convinced.*

*Within five years, the Cherokee nation adopted Sequoyah's syllabary as its official writing system. Beyond his life, this simple and lame man's work led to the creation of syllabaries for many other ethnic groups, including the Cree syllabary used by the largest group of First Nations people in Canada, Liberian syllabaries used in West Africa, and another syllabary used in China. Over all, Sequoyah's work influenced the creation of twenty-one writing systems for more than sixty-five languages. It is believed that the Austrian biologist Stephan Endlicher, who was also a linguist, named the Sequoia trees in California after the man who created talking leaves for his people.*

## A WORD CLUSTER

desmadre
enredo
e daí

Earlier, we explored the Japanese word for emancipation, *todatsu*, which means "a fish slipping out of the net." This word unfolds the struggle we face when we are the fish needing to free ourselves. Here, we will explore our struggle when we are the ones casting the net.

For this, I turn to the work of a leading peace builder, John Paul Lederach. In his early work in Mexico, he asked the people of a fishing village what words they use to say they are in conflict. After forty minutes of lively talk, they came up with two Spanish words for conflict: the word *desmadre*, which means "motherless, without a mother" and the word *enredo*, which means "the net is tangled." In the lineage of fishermen in Mexico, resolving conflict is the art of untangling the net, so they can fish again with the help of the Great Mother.

In such a village, fishing in the deep is how people feed themselves. And so, the net is essential to survival. When a physical net is actually tangled, the fishermen resolve the tangle by backing away from each other in order to stretch the net out between them. This way they can see where the tangle or knot is. Then, the knot is loosened or the patch of tangled net replaced. At worst, a new net is woven between them.

This has profound implications for how we might resolve

conflict between us. For conflict interrupts our ability to fish in the deep, and conflict prevents us from feeding on what is essential. The wisdom of the fishermen in Mexico tells us that, rather than being drawn into animosity over the conflict, it is imperative to back away from each other far enough to gain perspective on the conflict. Then, we can see where the tangle is between us. Then, we can go about undoing the knot or splicing a new patch of net. Or, if need be, we can weave a new net.

It is important to note that in identifying where the net is tangled, there is no time wasted on blame. The focus is on finding the tangle and undoing it, which requires regaining a broader perspective of the relationship and how the conflict has arisen.

There is another indigenous practice aimed at finding our way forward when we are troubled or confused or in conflict with life itself. This comes from the indigenous tribes of Brazil. When doing work in South America for the CDC, my dear friend David Addiss encountered the phrase *e daí* (ay-die-ee), which is Portuguese for "And then?"

Regardless of the story told or hardship conveyed, the custom is for the listener to say nothing but to ask after listening, "E daí?" with a tone that implies, "And so? What now?" Literally, *e* is "and" and *daí* means "from there, from a place near you."

The phrase *e daí* is invoked with three successive meanings, asked in three successive ways by the one who is hearing you out:

- The first utterance implies, *I hear what life has given you. E daí? And so, what does this mean? What does this matter?*
- The second utterance implies, *I see where you are. E daí? And so, from there, what is in front of you? What is just beyond where you are?*
- And the third utterance implies, *E daí? And so, what now? What is your next step?*

In a spiritually practical way, this custom invites us to locate ourselves in any given situation from the largest frame of reference possible to the immediate circumstance:

- Before we overreact or react prematurely to whatever situation we find ourselves in, it helps to ask, *E daí? What does this mean in the journey of your life, in its time on Earth, within the larger journey of all life across all time?* Such consideration will affect whether we respond at all or in what way.
- After locating the event in the largest frame, it helps to look at the particular situation and determine, *E daí? Given where you are, where is the next spot of solid ground? Will the ground beneath you bear your weight? Should you back up or move forward? Should you sidestep the situation? Or should you stand firmly where you are?*
- Finally, both the larger and more particular context help us to ask, *E daí? And so, what is your next step?*

I invite you to practice the custom of *e daí* with regard to a pressing situation in your own life. I invite you to explore this with a trusted friend or loved one. Have one of you ask and listen to the other, asking *e daí* in the three different ways. Then switch roles.

Both of these anonymous customs—*untangling the net* and *what is your next step?*—help us undo the knots between us and help us discover the path unfolding in our journey. It's humbling and astonishing that these spiritually practical efforts have accumulated their wisdom by word of mouth through the ages. If they speak to you, I encourage you to share these practices with others in your life.

## *A Question to Walk With*

In your journal, describe a significant relationship for you in which you are experiencing conflict. Tell the story of your bond with this person and the conflict that has arisen. Without blame, describe in detail the tangle between you. Later, go to this significant other and say without blame, "I think our net is tangled. Do you think our net is tangled? Where do you think it is tangled? And how might we undo the knot between us?"

## Our Conversation Over Time

*Earlier, I mentioned the beginnings of the* Oxford English Dictionary, *that massive communal undertaking of gathering a definitive compendium of the English language as it is actually used. There is another story embedded in that journey that chronicles a sheer devotion to words and an unlikely, lifelong connection that such a reverence spawned. I'm referring to the twining of Sir James Murray's life with the life of the American surgeon William Chester Minor. Their story is compellingly told by Simon Winchester in his novel* The Professor and the Madman, *which I also quoted earlier.*

*As a young man, James Murray had an exceptional gift for languages. He was fluent in English, Latin, Spanish, Catalan, Italian, and French and had a working knowledge of at least fourteen other languages. Though the meeting that conceived of the* Oxford English Dictionary *took place in 1857, it wasn't until March of 1879 that Murray signed an agreement to be its chief editor. Under his charge, the* OED *project would receive slips of paper with word origins and definitions from scholars and lay readers from around the world.*

*One of those contributors was William Minor, who had been psychically damaged as a Union surgeon in the Civil War. After being released from St. Elizabeth's Hospital in Washington, DC, Minor moved to London to recuperate from the war. It was there that Minor shot and killed an innocent man in what would probably have been termed today an incident of post-traumatic stress. Minor was found not guilty by reason of insanity and sent to Broadmoor Asylum in Crowthorne, where he spent the rest of his life.*

*Over a twenty-year period, Murray noticed that Minor stood out as the single most influential and constant contributor to the* OED, *having helped to define more than ten thousand words. In 1899, Murray acknowledged Minor's enormous contributions to the dictionary, stating publicly, "We could easily illustrate the last four centuries from his quotations alone."*

*Though the two lexicographers never met, the professor and the madman were bound together for much of their lives around the quest to create a lasting version of the English language for generations to come. Neither would see the completion of the* OED, *as both died before its publication in 1928. And unlike the Egyptian slaves who were embedded in the pyramids with their pharaoh, and unlike the conscripted Chinese workers whose very bodies were buried in segments of the Great Wall of China, Sir James Murray and William Chester Minor willingly poured their passion, sweat, and endless curiosity into the twenty volumes of the* OED, *which today spans more than twenty-one thousand pages and includes almost three hundred thousand words.*

## A WORD CLUSTER

### Eshu
### Ganesh

In the African Yoruba tradition, there is a deity known as Eshu, whose name means "the way opener." He is the god of experience who speaks all languages, implying that listening in all directions is the secret gift of the way opener. It's also implied that listening in all directions is crucial to uncovering the gift that lives within each of us.

Eshu has many names, including A-bá-ni-wá-ọ̀ràn-bá-ò-rí-dá, which means "He who creates problems for the innocent." Not as an agent of mayhem, but so the innocent can gain experience. In this way, Eshu is akin to the Hindu deity *Ganesh*, who is both the provider and remover of obstacles. Both Eshu and Ganesh cast obstacles as teachers and so, leave them in our path until we grow from encountering them. In the Judeo-Christian tradition, we pray to saints and sages to get us out of trouble. But in the African and Hindu traditions, the same god provides and removes the very obstacles we labor with.

By moving through the lessons that obstacles offer, Eshu is the one who teaches us that there are always two or more sides to every issue. It's this acceptance of many views that leads us to an awakened life. By deepening and broadening our perspective, the way opener introduces us to many pathways, all of which we're asked to live with. This defies our pressing want for the one path that will save us.

In Hindu mythology, Ganesh is typically depicted as an elephant with four giving hands. Ganesh is the Lord of all Beings. Legend has it that when given the task to race around the Earth, Ganesh did not traverse the outer surface of the planet, but simply walked *inwardly*, returning to the Center of All Existence, and calmly back to the surface where we live.

This is the secret understanding of Ganesh as the provider and remover of obstacles. For all too often, the obstacles we experience are presented as ways to remember that the inner walk through the Source, not the outer race, is the purpose of living. In this way, obstacles are often presented to break our trance with the race and jar us back to the Source. Humbly, the obstacles are often removed once our deeper sense has been restored.

We experience Eshu and Ganesh in our daily lives when we can see obstacles as unexpected teachers. When met openly and honestly, these teachers show us how to break our trance with the races we create and how to put down what we carry in order to live more directly and fully.

Another tale central in the life of Ganesh is that he himself was so irritated by an obstacle that he broke off one of his tusks and threw it in anger at the moon. And the moon, laughing, spit it back at him. And so, the very god of obstacles carries his broken tusk as a reminder that even the god of obstacles is not exempt from obstacles.

What broken piece do you carry to remind yourself that you are not exempt from the life of obstacles? How does returning to the Source remind you to listen in all directions? And how does listening in all directions reintroduce you to your gifts, which, in time, can mend the break?

## *A Question to Walk With*

In your journal, describe an obstacle that is currently in your face. How are you struggling with it and what do you think it is asking you to learn? Later, in conversation with a friend or loved one, discuss your history with Eshu, the way opener, and Ganesh, the provider and remover of obstacles. What deeper ways of being have obstacles opened in you over time?

## Our Conversation Over Time

*Earlier, we unpacked the word* holm *(pronounced "home") as an island in the middle of a stream or river. One of the crippling missteps in our human journey is when we lose our way from that abiding sense of home. This is the inner version of being homeless or holmless, which means being lost to our center and to the Center of Life. When we are led astray by pain or confusion or the unheralded strain of life's journey, we can lose our sense of home and be battered by the currents of the river.*

*A powerful example in nature is the Bengal tiger, whose native home is in the Sundarbans National Park, a large coastal mangrove forest that spans parts of India and Bangladesh. This rare, untouched coastal forest is also home to other endangered species, such as the primordial flying fish. The Sundarbans has always been a version of Eden for Bengal tigers. Only when tigers stray from their native home and are unable to find their way back do they become man-eaters. Likewise, only when we become holmless and can't find our way back to the Oneness of Life do we become cruel and violent.*

*No matter the length or curve of our journey, nothing is more crucial than to find our way back to the island in the center of the stream, where the soul knows it is home, regardless of the upheaval of circumstance that might surround us. This is how we practice inner restoration.*

## A WORD CLUSTER

haggadah
mwaramutse
ononharoia
mystery

In Hebrew *haggadah* means "telling"—in particular, telling the story of the liberation of the Jews from slavery in Egypt. More deeply, haggadah can be understood as the telling of any story of liberation from bondage, internal as well as situational. Part of that liberation is the telling of that story, so it can continue to unfold.

Where are you, then, in the story of your own liberation? To understand this, you must first understand the condition of your own bondage. What confines you? What holds you back? What keeps you from drinking from the light of your soul and the world?

I invite you to describe the condition of your bondage and its genesis. Then, I invite you to tell your own story of liberation—from a confining sense of self or from the confining mistreatment of others. Tell your own story and let the truth of your life unfold. For telling a truth story is great medicine.

Once you have uncovered the history of your bondage and wherever you are in the liberation of yourself, share the entire journey with a friend or trusted loved one. Let them bear witness to the truth of your journey. For bearing witness is part of the medicine, too. It is the telling and the bearing witness that let us wake and begin again.

After the genocide in Rwanda of the Tutsi people by the Hutu army in 1994, the common greeting among survivors became *Mwaramutse*, which means "Did you wake?"

Always, on the other side of suffering, we meet as survivors, asking: "Did you wake? Did you make it through? Did you find a way to begin again?"

So often, waking and beginning again involves undoing the patterns of our woundedness. In the Iroquois culture, the ononharoia, which means "turning the brain upside down," is an annual dream-walking festival during which the tribe opens itself beyond the ordinary thinking of daily life.

The festival begins with dream renewal, a time when those who were cured of illness during the past year offer dances for the health of those who helped heal them. Then there's time for dream sharing, when members of the tribe share dreams that have changed them or which they don't yet understand. Finally, there's *the* Ceremony of the Great Riddle, in which the shamans of the tribe attempt to interpret the shared dreams as instructions for the larger community.

We can benefit from these indigenous traditions of dream renewal and dream sharing as ways to turn the patterns of our brains upside down in order to erase them and begin again.

The telling of our bondage and liberation, the sharing

of how we wake from suffering, and the interpretation of dreams as instructions for our path forward—these are all inner rituals that help us return to the Mystery of Life.

This great, nameless resource is hidden in the open by our distortion of what we think mystery means. If you walk into any bookstore today, you will find a section labeled *mystery*. With utter innocence, you might think, this is where I can explore the depth and quandaries of what it means to be alive. But you will quickly find yourself surrounded by tales of murder and the endless variations of how we might solve the murders.

Sadly, while the original sense of mystery points to the inexplicable and ever-renewable Source of Life, the modern sense of mystery represents a genre solely devoted to the art of murder and the detective work necessary to solve the schemes that take life away. The devolved, modern sense of mystery is trying to solve the many ways we suffer loss of life, while the original sense of mystery renews our relationship to Source and all that we are given at birth.

What an odd turn of meaning across the centuries. Most critics and scholars credit Edgar Allan Poe with creating the first modern mystery with his short story "The Murders in the Rue Morgue," which featured C. Auguste Dupin as literature's first detective. Published in the April 1841 issue of *Graham's Magazine*, the story weaves the tale of an amateur detective who sets out to solve the grisly murders of a mother and daughter within a locked room of their apartment on the Rue Morgue.

Nearly twenty years later, Wilkie Collins published *The Woman in White* (1859), which is considered the first mystery novel, and *The Moonstone* (1868), considered the first detective novel. *The Woman in White* is an archetypal tale of murder, madness, and mistaken identity.

*The Moonstone* established the detective novel formula. The story centers on an enormous diamond, which is stolen from a Hindu temple and resurfaces at a birthday party in an English manor. With numerous narrators and suspects, the story finds its way to solve the puzzle.

In 1886, Robert Louis Stevenson published the classic mystery *The Strange Case of Dr. Jekyll and Mr. Hyde*, where a doctor of eminence is doomed to an uncontrollable transformation into a being of pure rage—repeatedly. This story explores our struggle with maintaining a proper, though unrealistic, public image while hiding our deeper impulses till they inevitably explode.

Yet, all the while, the deeper, more original sense of mystery lifts us, though it remains beyond our understanding. This deeper form of mystery brings us into our relationship with the unknown, into our relationship with everything larger than us, and into our relationship with everything that is life-giving, though it defies being named.

As Einstein beautifully expressed:

> *The most beautiful experience we can have is the mysterious. It is the fundamental emotion which stands at the cradle of all true art and science. Whoever does not*

*know it and can no longer wonder, no longer marvel, is as good as dead, and his eyes are dimmed.*

This is the true mystery to be solved and repaired: the disappearance of wonder. What clues must we trace to recover our direct and ineffable reverence for life? For through wonder, we recover the felt meaning of being here.

The word *mystery* comes from the Latin *mysterium* and refers to the notion of a *mystic*, which comes further from the Greek *muein*, which means "to close the eyes or lips [in order] to initiate."

The deeper sense of mystery, then, invokes an initiation into the inner realms of experience, which begins when we stop looking outward and begin to look inward. This is why many mythologies have an archetypal soothsayer, or truth-seer, who is usually blind or deaf, in order to enable them to listen and see more completely into the Source Energies of Life without being distracted by the noise of the outer world.

All forms of meditation help us limit the noise of the outer world, so we can receive the Mystery of the Inner World more completely. For stilling the noise of circumstance allows us to inhabit the Mystery more than solve it.

So, which form of mystery is calling you: the effort to solve the ways that life is taken from us, the effort to solve the ways that we murder our own energy, or the effort to re-establish our kinship with the Source of Life, the effort to inhabit the waterways of meaning that exist beyond our understanding?

The truth is that we need to be skilled at both. But unless the clues lead us to the Source, all attempts at solving mysteries are useless.

## *A Question to Walk With*

In your journal, describe which form of mystery has your attention: the mystery of how some aspect of life has been taken from you or the mystery of how the inexplicable Source of Life keeps speaking to you? Later, in conversation with a friend or loved one, discuss the things in your life that murder your energy and the things in your life that give you energy, and what you do to feed each of these forces.

## Our Conversation Over Time

*Another phrase that is part of my spiritual vocabulary comes from my cancer journey in my early thirties. The heat of that journey spanned three years during which I was thrashed about, in and out of hospitals, and in and out of surgeries and treatments. The journey to being here today was never straight or clear. Each turn of the journey felt abrupt and unpredictable. After a while, I started to see the ups and downs as a continual rhythm. Shortly after this, I chanced to see a dolphin break surface in the ocean. It was then that I named the rhythm of ups and downs the Dolphin Miracle.*

*For during my journey through cancer, the ribbon of life-force that kept showing itself in time to keep me going was like a dolphin, out of view in the deep, though breaching in the light at the most unexpected times. Just in time to save me, one more time. My life became tethered to the Dolphin Miracle. This has been my symbol for faith ever since.*

*Once out of the hospital and back in the stream of ordinary days, an old friend gave me a wooden dolphin made of dark mahogany. Oddly, it had one stripe of lighter wood along the dolphin's flank, as if it were mirroring the rib I had lost. It is in my bookcase behind me as I write this—a word-symbol of my journey. I hold it sometimes and close my eyes, feeling blessed to be here at all.*

## A WORD CLUSTER

santosha
sublime
suffer

In Sanskrit, the word *santosha* combines the word *sam* which means "completely, altogether, entirely" with the word *tosha* which means "contentment, satisfaction, acceptance." Santosha implies an inner state of equanimity that comes from accepting the circumstances of reality without denying their impact.

This inner state is an earned quality of being that does not try to flee the path of being human, while not being oppressed by the difficulties of being human.

Though no one quite knows how to do this, it is by engaging the spiritual mood of santosha that we don't try to alter or stop the Wheel of Life, nor do we acquiesce to all that befalls us. We participate fully by holding nothing back while accepting that we are subject to forces larger than us. This paradox—of being alive in the world by both engaging and accepting what life brings us—requires an inner skill that is difficult to inhabit but deeply worth pursuing.

To both engage and accept is how a tree grows while staying where it is. It's how a bird flies but always lands. To both engage and accept is how a human life depends on the sanctity of our heart to transcend our pain and yet, our heart can't exist unless it has a body to live in that registers our pain.

This brings us to the word *sublime*. While the common understanding of something sublime is that it contains unparalleled beauty, the root of the word comes from the Latin, which means "up to the threshold." So when something exhibits unparalleled beauty, that beauty of is-ness is a threshold to Wholeness, the way something illuminated by the sun shines in a way that leads us to the sun. And so, any living thing that reveals a threshold to Wholeness is sublime. And any depth that breaks our sense of what's familiar is also sublime. Awe is often the feeling awakened when experiencing the sublime.

Yet we can be brought *up to the threshold* of Wholeness by both great love and great suffering, by being made whole or by being broken open. In this regard, it's not by accident that the root of the word *suffer* means "to feel keenly."

For the lessons of life show us quickly that to know love and beauty, you must also feel keenly. Ultimately, it's the depth of sensitivity that suffering and love opens in us that allows us to access the Unitive Whole of Life. This unending depth is what's life-sustaining. As the great poet of the interior Rainer Maria Rilke said, "Let everything happen, beauty and terror. No one feeling is final. Keep going."

It's the inhabited life of feeling, opened by suffering as well as joy, that allows us to engage in life while accepting the larger forces that shape us. It's the authentic leaning in to what comes our way that lets us keep going, that lets us break what is familiar and habitual so we can drink from the sublime that underlies all of existence with its miracle of being.

A flower can't grow unless it has a root that is drinking from the soil. In just this way, a life filled with feeling can't grow unless it's gathering strength from the root of all being. And this vibrant, eternal depth empowers us to blossom in the human journey, while not being oppressed by being human.

## *A Question to Walk With*

In your journal, describe a recent moment that you felt keenly. Was it a moment of great love or great suffering? What threshold did feeling keenly lead you to? Later, in conversation with a friend or loved one, discuss your journey in engaging and accepting life.

## Our Conversation Over Time

*The Danish notion* hygge *(pronounced hue-gah) comes from a Norwegian word meaning "well-being." The word, which first appeared in Danish in the eighteenth century, suggests coziness. As a practice of community, hygge refers to the atmosphere we create between us. The Danish practice of hygge invites us to create well-being by evoking connection, warmth, and a sense of belonging. In Denmark and Norway, hygge refers to "a form of everyday togetherness"; "a pleasant and highly valued everyday experience of safety, equality, personal wholeness, and a spontaneous social flow." What, then, can you do in the coming days to create connection, warmth, and a sense of belonging with those you meet?*

## A WORD CLUSTER

reliable
contradiction
discipline
acceptance

In the stream of life, which is ceaselessly unpredictable, it's important to find a sense of what is reliable, that which is steadfast, constant, and enduring. The word *reliable* comes from the Latin *religare*, which means "to bind." The original sense of being reliable was "to bind together" because things and people are stronger when joined than when separate. In time, the sense of what is reliable evolved into "depending on someone or something with confidence."

In modern times, we've mistaken consistency for reliability. So often, I am considered reliable if I don't change, if my character remains the same. But this doesn't allow us room to grow. In his majestic poem "Song of Myself," Walt Whitman said, "Do I contradict myself? Very well then I contradict myself. I am large, I contain multitudes."

In truth, the heart of being reliable centers on how constant we can be in showing up for each other. It doesn't matter how much I change as I grow, but whether I will be there for you when you fall or lose your way. In this regard, our consistency of character is a facsimile of reliability. For every soul needs the space and depth to change and grow. In this, reliability is a matter of relationship and not maintaining a checklist of character traits.

To better understand the trap of consistency, we need to look more closely at the notion of contradiction. The word comes from the Latin *contra dicere* which means "to speak against." The word has come to mean "denying the truth by asserting the opposite." Yet, most things appear opposite or contrary because we are viewing them too close. When stuck in our closeness, we deem what is close as true and what is far as false.

Up close, a hummingbird's flight seems erratic, darting up and down and even sideways with no pattern. But when we back up, we can see a rhythm to the hummingbird's flight. Likewise, up close, falling seems the opposite of getting up, closing seems the opposite of opening, light seems the opposite of dark, and even life seems the opposite of death.

But when we enlarge our perspective, we begin to see the interconnected rhythm between these nodes of experience, which are not contrary but yielding of a Greater Whole. Now we begin to enter the world of paradox, where the ten thousand things of the world are only contradicting each other when we are too close to see the deeper truths that join them. When brave enough to step back into the realm of our unknowing, we begin to sense and feel the rhythm of how all things are true.

Our ability to discern what is truly reliable—what is truly steadfast, constant, and enduring—depends on whether we narrow or broaden our perspective. The aperture of our perception determines how deeply we learn.

The word *discipline* comes from the Latin *disciplina* which means "instruction [of] knowledge." While certain aspects of life are enhanced by our effort to sort through and focus on what's before us, there's a deeper, more lasting sense of understanding that comes from letting things in and seeing how they go together.

Too often, the single-mindedness of common discipline is exclusionary of what's next to learn, which by definition is beyond what we can see. So, a deeper sense of discipline arises, not by narrowing our focus, but by enlarging the sweep of our perception, so we can relate to what has always been but which we have yet to consider. And so, the spiritual sense of discipline is to open beyond what is familiar, so we can meet our next teacher.

All these efforts—to be truly reliable, to broaden our perspective, and to let things in and see how they go together—contribute to our practice of *acceptance*, which comes from the Latin *acceptare*, which means "to take something to oneself."

The practice of acceptance, then, is how we take life into us by meeting things as they are, how we meet life as clearly and truthfully as possible. Ultimately, acceptance is not static, not an act of resignation, but a dynamic, ongoing act of surrender and cooperation with the forces that are larger than us.

Acceptance is how a fish finds the current and aligns with it, swimming fully in rhythm with the river or sea that is carrying it. How, then, are you being asked to practice acceptance? How are you aligning and cooperating with the forces of life that are greater than you? What are you specifically being asked to look at truthfully and how are you being asked to embrace that aspect of life?

## *A Question to Walk With*

In your journal, tell the story of someone who has truly been reliable in your life, regardless of how they may have changed over the years. Later, in conversation with a friend or loved one, discuss where you are in your own practice of acceptance. What are you currently being asked to accept and what stands in your way?

## Our Conversation Over Time

*Watching the orange leaves let go and drift to the ground is a humble reminder of our struggle to hold on and let go as we drift through the days. The light in spring makes the leaves sprout until they grow so thick that they block the very light that brings them into being. Then, as the seasons pass, the leaves turn brilliant and finally let go. As if the end of all brilliance is to let go and become bare. So that the light can come through again.*

*This is like the journey of language over a lifetime. For words are like leaves and their language is their tree. The words sprout out of us when we can stay in the light. Then, mysteriously, paradoxically, the words grow into ideas and concepts that, in time, block the very light and source that gave us those words in the first place. Finally, if devoted to what words point to, the simplest of them turn brilliant like leaves in fall. And then we shed them, to let the light in again. So, words, like leaves, obey their seasons. And we are blessed to grow full and bare, again and again, learning from the life of words that grow out of us.*

### A WORD CLUSTER

#### trellis

The word *trellis* shares the same root with the word *rule*. A trellis is a temporary latticework, screen, or piece of upright wood that a vine, plant, or sprouting tree is tied to, so it has something sturdy to lean on and grow alongside until it can grow on its own. Then, the trellis is removed.

And so, the more helpful, original definition of a rule is not a confining restriction of behavior but a temporary structure that can help us grow. This is the enduring and healthy definition of a rule.

This notion is helpful in thinking about how to support our own growth and transformation. When trying to change or deepen our patterns in the world, it helps to create some form of structure in our days that we can lean on until the new behavior takes hold as a new way of being. And the new growth must not be tied too tightly to the trellis or it will be choked of its life and wither.

With regard to structures that human beings can grow alongside, a trellis or rule will surely be confining if it's imposed by another and only beneficial if such a temporary structure is self-created.

What, then, makes a good trellis for the growth of the soul? And how can we—as a parent, teacher, or friend—construct a good trellis out of our care? How can we support each other in our growth and remove our influence when those we love are strong enough to grow on their own?

## *A Question to Walk With*

In your journal, describe one way you want to change and grow. Then, imagine a steadying structure you can create in your days that will serve as a trellis or temporary rule you can grow alongside until the new behavior or way of being is strong enough in you to grow on its own. It might be taping a reminder on your mirror or setting aside a certain time every day to journal or meditate. Finally, take a first step in creating this trellis in your daily life. Later, in conversation with a friend or loved one, discuss the difference, as you've experienced it, between having a rule or structure imposed on you and when such a rule or structure has been self-created.

# The Work and Practice of Being Alive

*The Hindu worldview takes us through the unfolding of a self into the interdependent mystery beyond a single self, where we find ourselves in each and every living thing. This is what the holy phrase* Thou Art That *means. The notion comes from the story in the* Chandogya Upanishad *of a humble father Uddalaka and his precocious son Svetaketu, who at an early age is chosen to apprentice with the holy Brahmins. As soon as Svetaketu begins to study, he has no use for his father. He looks down on his simplicity and never asks him a question. One day, his father interrupts him, and Svetaketu impatiently asks, "What do you want, Father?"*

*Uddalaka says, "I want you to come with me." He leads his begrudging son to the foot of the great Nyagrodha tree. He picks a fruit and gives it to his son to hold, then asks him, "What do you see?" His son curtly answers, "Nothing. I see nothing." His father asks him to break open the fruit, which Svetaketu does; and they can see the seeds inside it. Again, his father asks him, "What do you see?" Again, his son says, "I see nothing, Father. Nothing!" Uddalaka opens a seed, which is hollow in the center, and puts it close to his son's face, and says, "Thou art that, my son, thou art that nothing."*

*More than putting his son in place, Uddalaka jars him to feel the great truth that we all come out of that unseeable center. We all grow from this great nothing, like the massive Nyagrodha tree. And so, the practice we're compelled to learn is how to face and feel a life of compassion that honors that we are at heart the same.*

*This chapter explores the wisdom in words that point to that unseeable center, words that for centuries have honored the mystical fact that we are at the heart the same, and what this means in our practice of being alive.*

## A WORD CLUSTER

### algebra

The mathematical sense of algebra comes from a book by the ninth-century Persian mathematician Al-Kwarizmi entitled *Kitab al-Jabr wa-l-Muqabala*, which means "the science of restoring what is missing and equating like with like." But the word *algebra* comes from the Arabic *al-jabr*, which means "the reunion of broken parts, bone-setting," and this comes from *jabara*, which means "to reunite, restore."

Life, by its very nature, is a reunion of broken parts. We begin Whole and, even in birth, are broken from the complete and unified consciousness of life as it exists before it enters all forms. So much of our journey through love and suffering is our return through experience to that mysterious Wholeness. And so, our struggles educate us in the algebra of truth.

This also speaks to the art of restoring what is missing, which is the human journey of a lifetime in falling down and getting up in order to become who we are. And equating like with like is at the heart of all metaphor, the great teacher that helps us navigate the paradoxes of life. In crucial ways, we are all students of the reunion of broken parts: within ourselves, between us, and in the constant repair of the world.

The ongoing work of self-awareness, then, is to discern where we are broken and what is missing. Then, life will present us with the inner curriculum that will lead us back to Wholeness. This ongoing practice opens us to the algebra of truth.

How can we do this in the days that are before us? We are all challenged to calm what is agitated and to stay connected to the pulse of life that is always below the agitation. No one knows quite where to begin, but we must try.

The reunion of broken parts depends on finding our place in the rhythm and cycle of life with all its expansions and contractions. Consider how the summer solstice is the longest day of the year. This recurring event in the life of our planet has always represented the cycle all humans move through, inwardly and outwardly, from dark to light, again and again.

As the planet keeps turning on its axis—turning away

from the light only to return to the light—so do we as spirits in bodies in time on Earth. By this turning, the Earth creates and sustains its seasons. As does the Life of Spirit.

This is a great teacher. For it is our commitment to keep turning to the light, day by day, that makes the awakening of the soul possible. It is our commitment to keep turning to the light, no matter what we encounter, that allows us to find what is missing and mend what is broken.

All these challenges to find what is missing and all these practices to mend what is broken are movements in the unrehearsable dance that is our life: growing, stumbling, becoming, finding out what's inside, and turning toward the light. Like a rock-climber in mid-reach or a dancer in mid-leap, the ever-deepening challenge is to practice life as it appears.

### *A Question to Walk With*

In your journal, describe a time when you turned away from the light and what caused you to do so. Then, describe how you turned back to the light and how this unfolded. If we turn from and to the light like the Earth in its orbit around the sun, how would you describe the central force that you orbit around?

## Our Conversation Over Time

*In the modern world, we are moving so fast that we tend to name things so as not to lose them. We name things to pin them down for a time when we might go back and look at them. We even name things to stop them from fleeing or chasing us. But the enduring, original effort to name things has always come after our experience of forces that have no names. We are ever called to experience the movement of things that matter and then to name them: as way to relate to them, as a way to incorporate these forces into our lives.*

*An affirming example of this original way of naming is still practiced in the West African Yoruba tradition, where a child is not named until its being is experienced, until the being, having come into the child, tells the parents the name by which it wants to be known. If we could only greet each other in this way, discovering each other's soul names after we experience each other.*

*In truth, wherever I go, life reveals its common center that can't be named. Once stopped in this way, there seems to be only one theme, though it comes in a thousand colors. As infinite songs are made of the same eight notes, there are a thousand ways to word the truth, though only one way to hear it. And the one theme, the one truth, the one place we are always opened to is the tender and indestructible breath of life. This is the treasure under everything we reach for and drop. It is under every pain, fear, word, and inside every patch of wonder. For being stopped makes us tender and simple.*

*My friend the poet Henk Brandt speaks to the want to be fully alive this way:*

No one knows
how I have struggled to become simple
as I aspire
to wade amidst the colors of the day
and be content

when radiance
sloughs off
being named.

For I would have myself be humble
and spend whole days
simply watching with my heart.

## A WORD CLUSTER

### tolerant

The word *tolerant* comes from the Latin *tolerare*, "to endure." Its meaning has evolved in many ways over time. In the 1580s, its original religious connotation implied "the action of allowing what is not approved." From the start, the stance of being tolerant was inherently arrogant and judgmental, allowing other views and traditions to exist, as long as they didn't aspire to an equal footing with the superiority of the tolerant one. From their perch of judgment, the superior one thinks of themself as magnanimous, while not approving of any tradition other than their own. This is a far cry from welcoming and accepting what is different from us.

In 1879, to be tolerant in the field of medicine described one's ability "to bear something without being affected" by it. This referred to a patient's ability to withstand pain and large doses of drugs. How much of the struggle or the cure can a person's system tolerate?

In the modern field of engineering, tolerance refers to the degree of strength and flexibility a material has to bend, withstand stress, and bear weight. This marks a building material's tolerance—such as steel, aluminum, iron, glass, or concrete.

But perhaps the most crucial form of tolerance refers to our inner capacity to find and deepen what is tolerable for us in how we move through the world. How do we become strong while staying tender, steadfast without shutting down? How do we move through the storms of life while staying vulnerable?

This sense of tolerance is not outward focused. It does not judge or test those around us. It is the inner work of integrity that allows us to stay close to life. And the range of our inner tolerance depends on how present, how centered, and how authentic we are in maintaining our kinship with all things.

In facing the religious and communal sense of tolerance, our attitude of "allowing what is not approved" needs to be dismantled in favor of a true welcome and acceptance of all that is different from us. Otherwise, we remain terribly isolated from everything. Yet by practicing true welcome and acceptance, we can move beyond the medical sense of tolerance, by which we bear something without being affected by it. This is inwardly important because, in the deepest of human ways, what good is being alive, if we're not affected by it?

Ultimately, being touched by what we encounter and being able to welcome and accept life that is different from us expands our strength and flexibility, allowing us to withstand stress and bear weight when necessary. Working with these combined practices of tolerance, in a truly personal way, makes life more tolerable, more bearable, more livable—without hardening our heart.

### *A Question to Walk With*

In your journal, describe the different ways you experience being tolerant: by allowing what is not approved; by bearing something without being affected by it; by expanding the degree of strength and flexibility you have to bend, withstand stress, and bear weight; and by developing your inner capacity to make life more bearable without losing your humanity. Which is a strength for you and which needs more of your attention? How can you inhabit these different forms of tolerance in a way that will bring your true self more alive?

## Our Conversation Over Time

*In my thirties, I underwent a very aggressive chemo treatment. During its last days, I was up in the night with painful attacks just above my stomach. They were debilitating and frightening. I learned later that the chemo was burning an ulcer in my esophagus. As these attacks escalated in the middle of the night, I struggled to demand and beg some form of guidance from God or any force to help me through. After the fourth sudden stab of pain, I somehow heard a disembodied, fleeting instruction that whispered to me from the inside, "Not thrones but zones."*

*It was strange and jarring, to say the least. Was it truly a voice or did the pain make me hallucinate? I wound up going to the emergency room and didn't recall this mysterious message till later the next week. It felt like my own little chemo-koan. The more I reflected on it, the more I came to realize that adjusting my entire perspective on life's journey was necessary for me to survive. No more seeking or plotting for thrones of accomplishment or esteem, but more, a devotion to inhabiting the zones of aliveness. This was profound. This slight distinction of words in the painful night was, indeed, a fork in the road: calling me to stop* pushing *my way through life in order to live life by* tending *to it. That was forty years ago and I can't tell you how vital and precious life has been since following the path of tenderness.*

## A WORD CLUSTER

authentic
forgive
dayenu

The word *authentic* comes from the Greek *authentes*, which means "bearing the mark of the hands." To be authentic is the art and practice of showing up.

Consider how the first thing to grow in the womb is the heart. And it's not by accident that our arms grow next as they sprout directly out of the heart. The early nubs that will be our arms look like tiny red wings, known as arm buds. Literally, the heart and hands are directly and forever connected.

This is why our arms move when we speak with passion. This is why we are warned of a heart attack by a sensation in our arm. We are considered integral when what we carry inside is congruent with our actions in the world. Integrity is the vow to keep trying to be authentic.

And so, when we bring what is in our heart through our hands into the world, we are authentic and real. How, then, can you practice being authentic in your days? How can you practice keeping your heart and hands connected?

Still, being human, we often miss where we aim. Things don't go as planned. We make mistakes. We break things we meant to carry carefully.

Because of our limitations, the practice of authenticity is forever paired with the practice of forgiveness, which is rooted in the practice of making amends. When those who hurt us won't own their trespasses, we are led more deeply into the struggle to forgive. What does this mean?

Without an acknowledgment of being hurt or betrayed, the work of forgiveness becomes internal work. It helps here to note that the word *forgive* means "to give for." While the repair of a relationship derailed by woundedness has its own journey, the deeper process of forgiveness within oneself implies a sense of exchange. But what are we exchanging and what for?

When wounded, it's natural to have a part of our heart devote itself to tending the wound. But as long as part of our heart is tied to the wound, we have less than a full heart to meet life with. Forgiveness, at its life-giving core, asks that we exchange the wounded part of our heart in order to regain the full use of our heart to live with.

This process can happen in a moment or take years, depending on the severity of the wound. There is no moral judgment attached to how long it takes to make the exchange. In truth, there is no arrival point. Being aware of this process and engaged in it is by itself forgiving.

By staying engaged in the work of being authentic and the work of exchanging our woundedness to regain the full use of our heart, we enter a deeper agreement with acceptance regarding the ups and downs of life.

This brings us to the Hebrew word *dayenu* which means "it would have been enough." More than a thousand years old, dayenu is a song sung at Passover. It's a song of gratitude sung in the midst of hardship. It was first sung by the Jews set free by Moses, who found themselves lost in the desert after leaving the bondage of Pharaoh. Dayenu has become a song sung by those washed ashore as they cough up the sea, just grateful to be alive.

In truth, the hardships we meet compel us to voice dayenu in the present tense: It *is* enough. After almost dying of cancer in my thirties, I felt a humble gratitude even for bad weather. Dayenu, it's enough to rejoice while caught in the rain. In truth, the only bad weather is no weather. Dayenu, it's enough to have one eye, if the other can't see. Dayenu, it's enough to admit I know nothing, when all I've learned has failed.

A personal example of struggling to be authentic, to forgive, and to accept centers around my lifelong journey with my father who's now gone. He was a master woodworker, a creative force. Though I was inspired by his creativity, we worked in such different mediums—he with wood, me with words—that we couldn't find a common language.

When he wouldn't show up for me during my cancer journey, we became estranged for seventeen years. His absence was a deep wound. But after being abandoned while near death, being authentic meant that I could only leave the door open and wait for him to come through.

During our years of estrangement, I felt a great deal, including, in time, the need to put all my grievances down in order to regain the full use of my heart.

Finally, when my father turned ninety, I wanted to see him. I rushed to meet him. When I parked in the driveway of the home I grew up in, this old man came teetering out the front door leaning on a cane. With tears in his eyes, he said, "I never thought I'd see you again." Then he dropped his cane and kissed me on the neck. Dayenu, that kiss was enough, like honey poured in our wounds. Dayenu, it was enough to receive his love, though we had lost so many years.

## *A Question to Walk With*

In your journal, describe a recent experience when what you felt in your heart made it through your hands into the world. What did this process feel like? How did it impact others? How did it impact you? Later, in conversation with a friend or loved one, discuss one particular moment of woundedness that is keeping you from living fully. How might you begin the process of reclaiming the full use of your heart?

## Our Conversation Over Time

*There are two unending practices that remain central to the work of being alive, which everyone has to personalize.*

*Earlier, we discussed the derivation of the word* war, *which traces back to its Indo-European root* wers, *which means "to confuse, mix up." This leads to the first unending practice we must inhabit, which is a devotion to clearing confusion, both within us and between us.*

*Along the way, we also discussed John Paul Lederach's research in Mexico into the indigenous ways of handling conflict. As he learned, the members of that fishing village described the process of resolving conflict as* enredo, *which means "untangling the net." This points to the second unending practice we must inhabit. For we are each left to discover how our nets are tangled and to stay devoted to untangling them.*

*Both the clearing of confusion and the untangling of nets are inner skills that, when engaged with as teachers, can change how we live on Earth.*

## A WORD CLUSTER

prajna garba
ginosko
honor

In Buddhism, *prajna garba* means "the womb of wisdom," which implies that wisdom must be brought full term and given birth to. This seems to say that the truth of our experience can only release its wisdom if we embody it. That is, we have to live our wisdom, one insight at a time, by meeting what comes our way and processing it.

Human beings are the only perceptual creatures that can comprehend something without inhabiting it. While this gives us an extraordinary intellectual reach, it also gives us the illusion that we have lived certain things when we haven't. To grasp something is not to live it. To comprehend something is not to experience it.

The aim of life is to be fully alive. And we can't live fully without enduring and engaging the labor necessary to birth our wisdom. The midwives of wisdom are often humility and acceptance. For no matter how grand our dreams, life will break us and ground us into exactly who and what we are. This can be devastating. Yet, in time, we come to see the magnificence of being ordinary and the blessing in being simple. We do not bend life but bend to it. Eventually, our life-lines and dream-lines coincide with what we are reduced to on the other side of our experience.

There are many ways to enter this process. Let me invoke two.

In Greek, *ginosko* means "to come to know, the recognition of truth by experience." This is the first practice in the labor of coming fully alive: to recognize truth as we distill it through our experience.

As impatient as we are, this distillation can only happen through time. Like it or not, time slowly exposes the story of our lives with its friction; wearing away the film that covers our eyes and the calluses that guard our heart, till we can apprehend the wonder waiting just under the skin of everything. Can we facilitate this process? I'm not sure, but we can ready ourselves.

The second practice in coming fully alive is to stay devoted to the act of honoring. I love the original meaning of the word *honor*, which is "to keep what is true in view." It's one of the most genuine and useful words I know.

I honor you, as a friend or loved one, when I keep what I know to be true about you in view, especially when you can't. I honor my own life-force when I keep what I know to be true about the nature of my soul in view. I honor life itself when I keep what I know about the Mysteries in view, though they can never be seen. The life of honor calls on us to befriend the many facets of life by bearing witness to the truths that move through us.

We stay fully alive by recognizing the verities as they are revealed in our experience and by keeping what is true in view. These practices uncover our wisdom as it comes full term. Both practices make us intimate partners with life over time. And to our surprise, the true end of wisdom is that we become what we seek.

## *A Question to Walk With*

In your journal, describe a significant experience you've been through and one insight of wisdom that you've distilled from it. Later, in conversation with a friend or loved one, discuss what you know to be true about each other. Give voice to these truths and practice honoring each other.

## Our Conversation Over Time

*The Lebanese greeting* ya ayuni! *literally means "Oh, my eyes!" or "Oh, my darling!" Implicit in this ancient greeting is the recognition that we need each other to see, that one view is insufficient. Empowered by the presence of each other, the Lebanese people say, "Oh, my eyes! You're here! Now we can see!" This custom reminds me of how Native American elders meet in a circle, not just for equity, but so that each elder will have a direct view of the Center. The belief at the heart of these elder councils is that the Center and the Whole are not comprehensible by any one person. No one view is enough. Therefore, we need everyone's view to glimpse the enduring truths of life. And so, we gather meaning, we don't choose it.*

*Ya ayuni! "Oh my eyes! You're here! Now we can see!" The sustaining lift of this custom—that we sorely need to enliven today—is to welcome other views in the belief that we need each other to be complete.*

## A WORD CLUSTER

pray
realize

The word *pray* comes from the Latin *precari*, which means "to ask earnestly." So prayer is tied to asking questions. Only in our desperation does it turn into asking for something particular. To pray is more deeply about listening than speaking, more deeply tied to asking for help in accepting what is than asking for a way out.

Ultimately, we are asked to listen beyond what we ask for, to keep our heart and mind open beyond what we think we need. Yet we still need to ask, for the asking opens us to what can truly help, which is the stream of life-force and Spirit looking to fill and renew all forms of life, if we give it a place to enter. It's the humanness of our prayer, whether we get what we ask for or not, that makes the opening for grace.

When exhausted of our urgency, we're laid bare beyond what we think we need. Once in this bare space with nothing between us and life, we're closer to the realm of all that is real.

This brings us to the word *realize.* In our overly mental modern world, we have thinned the meaning of the word to mean "to become fully aware of, to comprehend" as in "I realized I was defensive all along." Yet the root of the word means "to make real."

And so, in essential ways, to pray is to listen so deeply that our bare perception lets things become real. To pray is to listen so deeply to what is that we remove whatever is in the way long enough to reclaim our Original Presence and kinship with life.

My own experience of this led me to retrieve this poem:

AT EVERY TURN

*When I sweat trying to lift*
*what no one can lift,*
*I am praying.*

*When I fly 1000 miles to be*
*stopped by the moon on the*
*spine of an ancient mountain,*
*I am praying.*

*When I fall on the lawn in laughter*
*with my dog and she won't stop*
*licking my face,*
*I am praying.*

*When you are winded by the light*
*on the photo of your mother*

*who died so suddenly,*
*you are praying.*

*When your grief lets you feel the*
*pain of those you don't know,*
*you are praying.*

*When life moves through us*
*for no reason,*
*we are all praying.*

*I am humbled that all my efforts*
*to pray have failed, until*
*living is praying*
*with no intent.*

*Now, my heart is plucked*
*like the string of a harp*
*at every turn.*

How, then, can we find the courage to listen beyond all our pleas until we're buoyed by the ground of being that carries us all? Not by bypassing our human need to ask for help. But to voice everything till we exhaust all our requests and are left in the bare space of life-force that only knows how to live. In truth, asking and putting down is an apprenticeship that wears us down till "living is praying with no intent," till we are "plucked like the string of a harp at every turn."

## *A Question to Walk With*

Practice praying by asking for what you need and keeping your heart and mind open beyond your asking. Until you are drifting in the raw field of true listening. Receive what is offered there, even if it defies your understanding. Afterward, journal in detail about your experiment with prayer. What did it feel like to ask for what you need? What did it feel like to listen beyond your asking? What did you hear and absorb once in the realm of true being? Is this helpful? How?

## Our Conversation Over Time

*In a time long gone, before the advances of technology, before language was precise, clans roamed the plains and slept in the mountains. And one day, while hunting for food, the elder of a clan saw his youngest in the sights of a lion. He quickly shouted a sharp, deep, guttural sound that both startled the lion and alerted the boy. From that time on, language was used as a form of protection in an unpredictable world. The next summer, the boy grew lost in wonder, watching clouds drift before the sun. When his father found him, he sat with him in the wonder and sighed a long, deep sigh that connected their souls to the clouds. From that time on, language was used as a way to affirm our kinship with everything larger than us.*

*In order to survive, we have to acknowledge that, as the German playwright Bertolt Brecht said, "Hunger is understood in any language." But in order to thrive, we have to surrender to the truth that the Japanese teacher Kukai offered when he said, "The first word, 'Ah,' blossoms into all others. Each of them is true."*

*It's also true that when we withhold the word, people forget how to survive or thrive. But when great love or suffering open us, the word like a nameless angel slips inside and people remember what a fragile, resilient miracle it is to be alive.*

## A WORD CLUSTER

regret
sacrifice

The word *regret* comes from the Old French word *regreter*, which means "one who bewails the dead," and this goes further back to the German root meaning "to greet." We always face these two phases of regret: to bewail what's gone wrong and what's been lost *and* to greet the chance to do things differently. The deeper practice of regret is to re-greet and re-meet the situations we have bungled, so we might make amends and course-correct.

While the mood of regret is often guilt, the purpose of regret is to do things differently. While the weight of regret can pull us into the past, the focus of regret is to better ourselves moving forward.

How, then, do we outlast our remorse in order to focus on how we might do things differently? The purpose of relationships that don't work is that they help us inhabit relationships that do. And the purpose of falling down is that we can practice getting up. And the purpose of dreams that don't come true is that they serve as kindling for the dream of who *we* are, helping *us* come true.

In my twenties, I went rock-climbing with my dear friend Paul, who was a master rock-climber. I felt compelled to experience this process. He tied me to him and went first, scaling a large, pronounced rock face before us. He was about twenty feet ahead of me when I slipped and slid down the rock, cutting up my arms and shins.

There I bobbed and dangled, my heart racing, the rope tight around my chest. When I came to a stop, I looked up at Paul. He called out, "Are you alright?" I nodded yes. And then, without hesitation, he motioned me to ascend where I had fallen—one more time. All these years later, I realize that this is the true practice of regret: to climb over the exact terrain of our mistakes—one more time. There is no other way forward.

This sense of course correction applies to the larger patterns of our life as well. This brings us to the original definition of the word *sacrifice*. We know sacrifice more commonly as the giving of one's self, even life, for the greater good. We think of soldiers sacrificing their lives to preserve our freedom. During the pandemic, we witnessed countless health-care workers sacrifice their well-being to bring us through.

Yet these noble efforts grow out of a more ancient soil of sacrifice. For the original definition of sacrifice is "to give up what no longer works in order to stay close to what is sacred." Inherent in its meaning is the spiritual fact that everything is sacred. It is we who move in and out of living in accord with that sanctity.

The implication is that what works today in keeping us close to what is sacred may not work tomorrow. Because, while the sacred doesn't change, we keep changing. And so, we're drawn into a lifelong practice of discerning what no longer works, so we can put it down and replace it with something new that will let us drink again from what is sacred.

It's important not to demonize what no longer works. After all, when a butterfly emerges from its cocoon, it doesn't mean the cocoon was false. Rather, it served its purpose. In just this way, old identities, dreams, beliefs, or relationships are sacred passages that we emerge from. They are not false, but developmental.

Growing up in a sarcastic, cutting household, I learned to deflect and fend off judgments and jabs without showing how they hurt me. This was necessary to survive adolescence.

But on the other side of my cancer journey, it was clear that I didn't survive to avoid the touch of life. And what once served as a protection was now isolating me from the tender vulnerability of being alive. Now, I had to put down this defensive reflex in order to be more fully alive.

The practice of regret helps us re-meet the awkward passages we have stumbled through, so we can be more skillful the next time. And the practice of sacrifice helps us set aside what no longer works, so we can regain our intimacy with all that is sacred.

While our aim is noble, our attempts to reach what we aim for are terribly human. And so, true regret and true sacrifice are the corrective practices that help us stay present, vital, and real.

## *A Question to Walk With*

In your journal, describe one action or lack of action you regret. Examine the situation closely, beyond any sense of guilt or remorse. Detail the ways you might re-greet and re-meet this situation differently. Begin to do so. Later, in conversation with a friend or loved one, discuss one way of being or feeling or thinking that is no longer working. How might you put it down in order to stay close to what is sacred? What might you replace this with?

## Our Conversation Over Time

*For years, I've been drawn to the Native American way of naming things, offering phrases from the natural world to point to what is unsayable. In trying to give voice to the inner life and its immeasurable sensations, this poem came through me:*

UTTERANCE-THAT-RISES-BRIEFLY-FROM-THE-SOURCE

Peace is an odd word for the bubble of all there is
breaking repeatedly on the surface of the heart,

but I know of no other. The Native Americans
come closest; nothing between inner events
and what to call them. I see you and you always
glow. Why not call you One-who-shines-like-a-
sun-upon-first-meeting. Why not call the moment
of doubt and fear: Dark-point-spinning-loose-
that-presses-on-the-throat. Why not call the
moment of certainty, the fleeting moment
when everything that ever lived is right
behind my pounding heart, why not call
that moment: Beat-of-the-thousand-wings-
of-God-inside-my-chest. When I feel love so
deeply that I can't bear it, when I feel it so much
that it can't be contained or directed at any one
thing or person, why not call it: The-stone-at-the-
bottom-of-the-river-sings. Why not call you: The-
hand-that-plucks-me-from-the-bottom-of-the-river.
Why not call this miracle of life: The-sound-that-
never-stops-stirring-the-lost-within-the-sound-that-
never-stops-soothing-the-living-within-the-sound-that-
never-stops-sounding-in-the-eyes-of-dead-things-coming-
alive-again-and-again-and-again . . .

*Notice how more and more of the poem is hyphenated. This came about quite naturally as the river of expression kept resisting the names I tried to put to it. So, I began to hyphenate more and more of the words, trying to stay faithful to the place where words surge from all that is wordless. In truth, words are like waves. They call us to the unnamable ocean of meaning from which they rise. Any one followed deeply enough will bring us home.*

## A WORD CLUSTER

mkeka
wa
doryoku
welcome
companion

In Swahili, *mkeka* means "the foundation of all knowledge and understanding that living together returns us to." This is at the heart of all spiritual traditions: formal or informal, ancient or modern, indigenous or reformed.

Despite the many paths to Oneness, it seems the only way to inhabit this journey is through the authentic living of the one life we are given. Experience alone, when endured and embraced, will bring us to this kind of living knowledge. No other destination is as crucial or lasting as the wisdom wrung out of our daily experience.

The ongoing question is how. In Japanese, *wa* means "harmony" and *doryoku* means "effort." Together, they suggest that the way we move through experience is to animate harmony through effort. But how do we make sense of our experience? Who and what do we listen to along the way?

How do we listen to life and not to what life does to us, when suffering and loss meet us at every turn?

We must never be ashamed of giving our all, no matter how awkward that effort may make us look. For it's the thoroughness of our humanity that makes the essence of life visible and drinkable.

The word *welcome* comes from a Scottish saying that means, "come to the well." When we greet each other at any threshold, we are saying, "Come to the well and drink. Come to the well, where we can effort our way together into the foundation of all knowledge that lets us know we are each other."

We do this by living the days together, by helping each other up and setting each other down, by listening to each other's joys and sorrows and the music our stories release. We do this by keeping each other company. So, let's be a *companion* to each other, which goes back to the French meaning "one who breaks bread with another."

It always comes down to this: our willingness to walk together through the storm and share what we have, so we can create a path to the lake of all that matters, where we can finally drink and rest.

## *A Question to Walk With*

In your journal, describe an experience of effort that led you to a moment of harmony. How did this happen? How has this impacted your understanding of effort and harmony? Later, in conversation with a friend or loved one, discuss what it means to be a good companion and imagine one step you can take to be a better companion to each other.

## Our Conversation Over Time

*I was wading with my eight-year-old niece in the August lake when a pair of mallards swam very close. We had nothing to feed them but our awe, and half thinking aloud, I told Jessica that* duck *was such a poor name for such a colorful creature. She thought awhile and then blurted out, "Featherbacks!" I looked at her. She splashed with glee and shouted, "We shall call them Featherbacks!" And I longed for her to look that way at me and couldn't imagine what name she might give to the thing in me that wants to dive and fly.*

### A WORD CLUSTER

komorebi

The Japanese word *komorebi* signifies "the shimmering of light and shadows [on a wall] created by leaves swaying in the wind." The pattern only exists on a surface once, at that moment. This is yet one more word that serves as an indelible placeholder for all that is ephemeral. It's a fitting word to share near the end of our inquiry.

For while what matters, what is sacred, is always present, its appearance to us is shimmering and fleeting. Only revealing itself in each moment, never replicated. Isn't this how insight after insight appears? Isn't this how love and truth appear? Something undeniable, like light, moves through something delicate, like our person, and the wisdom that appears slips through all our defenses to waver on the tender inch we show no one. Words can do this. Listening can do this. You and I slowing each other down can do this.

Perhaps every word is a form of komorebi. Perhaps what we experience shimmers its lesson, like light and shadow, on the altar of our heart, where it nudges us to stop and fully be here, one more time.

## *A Final Question to Walk With*

In your journal, describe three words that have been great teachers for you. Later, in conversation, introduce these great teachers to a friend or loved one. Then, try to agree on a spirit name for your friendship.

# Honey Guides

the African greater honey guide

*In the beginning of this book, I mentioned the African bird known as the greater honey guide that leads tribal members to the honey in beehives. All words are such guides that can lead us to the honey hidden in life. I encourage you to go back to the honey guides in this book that have touched you and spoken to you. Spend more time with them. Let them guide you. And beyond this book, try to put aside your assumptions and conclusions and enter your days looking for the honey guides that are waiting for you.*

*If we look closely, there are two more lessons we can glean from the greater honey guide. Left to its own native disposition, a honey guide will attract a person's attention with a wavering chatter from its beak. They actually want to lead the hunters to the honey. And honey hunters will call the guiding bird as well. In Boran, honey hunters use a loud whistle to call the honey guide. In Mozambique, honey hunters utter a* brrrr-hmm *call.*

*So, the first lesson is that we must listen for the call of what matters and offer a call ourselves for what is essential and lasting. In our relationship with words, this means we must listen for the ring of truth wherever it might appear, for the words want to lead us to their meaning, and we must call the truth into the open by voicing the words themselves wholeheartedly. Words will not come alive if we do not voice them. And words will not guide us if we are not present.*

*The second lesson centers on gratitude over manipulation. While some tribes try to starve the honey guide, thinking that to keep the bird hungry will make it lead them to more beehives, other tribes experience greater yield and abundance when they leave a gift of honey for the bird. For gratitude is more of a way opener than manipulation. We simply must share the honey we find in life. It's the only way.*

*All this brings us to the language of birds, which in many cultures is seen as a mystical language of Unity and Wholeness. Mythically, birds are used as messengers of what matters. The language of birds is symbolic of the power of words to reveal the enduring yet intangible qualities of life.*

*In Norse mythology, Odin has two ravens who fly around the world and come back to teach him from all that they see. Odin's ravens represent the power of words to expand our consciousness. In the Jataka tales, which tell the stories of Buddha's previous lives in human and animal form, he often appears as a bird bestowing lessons. In biblical lore, the wisdom of Solomon and David is deepened because they have been taught the language of birds. And in the legendary*

*Sufi poem by Attar "The Conference of Birds," the birds of the world gather to uncover the flaws and patterns that prevent human beings from attaining enlightenment. All this tells us that words, like birds, are alive, always moving between our life on Earth and the Heavens.*

*The truth is that no matter what keeps us from being fully here, it is the language of the soul, the awakening power and medicine of words, that can restore us. And so, we end where we began, with the attribution of Buddha, under the stars, instructing his students by saying, "My words are only fingers pointing at the moon. Make sure you look at the moon!"*

*I implore you to look at what the words in your life point to. Let the language of the soul usher you into the River of Aliveness. Let the language of the heart usher you into the ever-nourishing Waterfall of Time. Let the language of kinship and kindness usher you into the Web of Relationship that holds the world together. Choose your words with care and they will love you into becoming who you are. Find the words that remove what's in the way and care for them and they will become the windows in your life that will let light in, day after day.*

# Gratitudes

I'm indebted to my good friend Karen Horneffer, who, over dinner in early spring a few years ago, encouraged me to put these word-teachers together in a book. I began gathering them the next day. And to my students, especially those in a yearlong journey in 2014 who offered me a list of the words I had unpacked for them throughout the year.

I am also deeply grateful to my agent, Eve Atterman, for her loving support through the years, and to James Munro and Fiona Baird and the WME team for putting my work in front of readers around the world. And to my publisher, Joel Fotinos, for his creative friendship and his deep openness of mind. And to Brooke Warner, my trusted friend, reader, and vision partner, for our many years of creating together, especially for helping me unravel the structure of this book. And to my publicist, Eileen Duhne, for representing me so well in the world.

Gratitude to my dear friends. Especially George, Don, Paul, Skip,

TC, David, Parker, Kurt, Pam, Patti, Paula, Ellen, Dave, Jill, Jacquelyn, Linda, Michelle, Rich, Carolyn, Henk, Elesa, Penny, Sally, and Joel. And to Oprah Winfrey for being such a deep listener. And to Jamie Lee Curtis for the fierceness of your care.

And to Paul Bowler for the long journey together. And to Robert Mason for being such a steadfast brother of Spirit. And to my dear wife, Susan, for the tender garden you are.

—MN

# Notes

## The Nature of the Soul

p. 20: **"the place of blessing . . ."** This paragraph first appeared in my book *The Book of Soul*. New York: St. Martin's Essentials, 2020, p. 6.

p. 20: **"Imagine Buddha . . ."** This passage first appeared in the entry for May 23 called "To Be Awake" in my book *The Book of Awakening*. Newburyport, MA: Red Wheel, 2020, p. 170.

p. 24: **"If we trace . . ."** This paragraph first appeared in my book *Finding Inner Courage*. Newburyport, MA: Red Wheel, 2010, p. 161.

p. 25: **"Olasope Oyelaran . . ."** This passage first appeared in my book *Seven Thousand Ways to Listen*. New York: Atria, 2012, p. 5. Dr. Oyelaran was the director of the College of Arts and Science in the School of International Studies at Western Michigan University. Born in Nigeria and educated in the United States, Dr. Oyelaran has been instrumental in higher education in Nigeria for many years.

p. 27: **"These choices are represented by the two prominent Buddhist traditions . . ."** I also refer to these traditions in my book *More Together Than Alone* (New York: Atria, 2018, p. 44), and in the chapter "Sympathetic Fibers" in my book *Finding Inner Courage* (Newburyport, MA: Red Wheel, 2010, p. 78).

p. 30: **"in West Africa, there is one word for being and doing, *iwa* . . ."** I first explored the word *iwa* in my book *The Endless Practice*. New York: Atria, 2014, p. 214. I am again indebted to the linguist Dr. Olasope Oyelaran for his deep knowledge of the Yoruba culture and language.

p. 32: **"The original countenance . . ."** From *Zen Buddhism: A History, Volume 2: Japan* by Heinrich Dumoulin. Bloomington, IN: World Wisdom Books, 2005.

## The Journey of Inwardness

p. 45: **"I cannot doubt that language . . ."** Charles Darwin, from *The Descent of Man, and Selection in Relation to Sex*, 2 vols. London: Murray, 1871, p. 56.

p. 46: **"These early mothers . . ."** Dean Falk, from "Prelinguistic evolution in early hominins: whence motherese?" in *Behavioral and Brain Sciences*, Issue 27, August 2004, pp. 491–503.

p. 46: **"Philip Lieberman had another theory . . ."** From "The Evolution of Human Speech: Its Anatomical and Neural Bases" in *Current Anthropology*, Issue 48, 2007, pp. 39–66.

p. 49: **"the Way of unifying (with) life energy"** From *The Principles of Aikido*, Mitsugi Saotome. Boston: Shambhala, 1989, p. 222.

p. 50: **"self-confidence."** I first explored this deeper notion of confidence in the April 14 entry of my daybook, *The Book of Awakening*. Berkeley, CA: Red Wheel-Conari Press, 2000 & 2020.

p. 52: **"The gall wasp lays her eggs . . ."** I am indebted to my dear friend Michelle Pensec Salyers, for teaching me about the oak gall, which she discovered in her work with thread and yarn. Please see colormehappyfiberarts.com.

p. 52: **"students in China."** I was teaching for the Hailan Family Well-Being peer education institute. And I am indebted to Dr. Hailan and Joy Huang Xiaoyu for their impeccable care and for inviting me to teach and journey with their community, and to my dear friend Paul Ginter for introducing us. Please visit hailanxfj.com. I first explored these learnings in my book *Falling Down and Getting Up*. New York: St. Martin's Essentials, 2023, pp. 21–23.

p. 56: **"The Chinese word *hsien* . . ."** Details of the root meaning of these words come from the glossary that David Hinton provides in his remarkable book of translation *Classical Chinese Poetry.* New York: Farrar, Straus and Giroux, 2008, pp. 447–450.

p. 59: **"the word *radical* . . ."** For a more in-depth exploration of what it means to be radical, see the chapter "To Be Radical" in my book *Surviving Storms*. New York: St. Martin's Essentials, 2022, p. 70.

p. 62: **"the word *sage* . . ."** For a more in-depth exploration of the history of sages, see the chapter "In the Presence of Sages" in my book *Seven Thousand Ways to Listen*. New York: Atria, 2012, p. 68.

p. 63: **"the effort of our sincerity . . ."** For a more in-depth discussion of sincerity, see the chapter "A Sincere Life" in my book *The Exquisite Risk*. New York: Harmony Books, 2005, p. 56.

p. 67: **"Yūgen . . ."** See *The Karma of Words*, William R. LaFleur. Berkeley, CA: University of California Press, 1986. He devotes an entire chapter to the word *yūgen*.

p. 67: **"On an autumn evening . . ."** the Japanese poet Chomei (1153–1216), cited in *The Karma of Words: Buddhism and the Literary Arts in Medieval Japan* by William R. LaFleur. Berkeley, CA: University of California Press, 1983, p. 99.

p. 68: **"narrow road to the interior . . ."** I highly recommend Sam Hamill's compelling translation *Narrow Road to the Interior and Other Writings,* Basho, translated by Sam Hamill. Boston: Shambhala

Publications, 2000. His introduction alone is company for the ages; offering insight into the life and formation of Basho's sensibility, while giving a history of the most sincere lineage of Japanese poetry.

p. 71: **"I offer four trusts . . ."** I first explored the four trusts in depth in my book *Finding Inner Courage*. Newburyport, MA: Red Wheel, 2010, p. 166.

## The Nature of Life

p. 79: **"Maya is the goddess of illusion . . ."** This description of Maya first appeared in my book *Seven Thousand Ways to Listen*. New York: Atria, 2012, p. 181.

p. 80: **"The Native Americans are wise teachers in this . . ."** An earlier discussion of "all my relations" first appeared in my book *The Endless Practice*. New York: Atria, 2014, p. 118. My evolving understanding of "all my relations" and other communal understandings cited throughout this book, such as ubuntu, thou art that, I-Thou, ya ayuni, the Great Spoked Wheel, hygge, and the African custom of "I see you! I am here!" culminated in the chapter "Eight Worldviews and Practices" in my book *More Together Than Alone*. New York: Atria, 2018, p. 323.

p. 82: **"In the Aztec culture of Central America . . ."** The Wikipedia article "Mythical Origins of Language" has been a remarkable resource in my recasting of these stories. See en.wikipedia.org/wiki/Mythical_origins_of_language.

p. 84: **"The legendary Chinese thinker Confucius . . ."** First cited in my book *Surviving Storms: Finding the Strength to Meet Adversity*. New York: St. Martin's Essentials, 2022, p. 135.

p. 84: **"To find the central clue . . ."** Confucius, *The Analects*. New York: Penguin Classics, 1998.

p. 85: **"The Buddhist word *haecceitas* . . ."** First cited in my book *The*

*Endless Practice: Becoming Who You Were Born to Be*. New York: Atria, 2014, p. 257.

p. 89: **"In the Taoist tradition . . ."** This paragraph first appeared in my book *The Book of Soul*. New York: St. Martin's Essentials, 2020, p. 161.

p. 93: **"Consider Shakespeare . . ."** These two paragraphs first appeared in the chapter "The Origins" in my book *Drinking from the River of Light*. Louisville, CO: Sounds True, 2019, p. 47.

## The Journey to Oneness

p. 101: **"Arthur Zajonc"** is a remarkable physicist and teacher who taught from 1978 to 2012 at Amherst College. He has worked with several Nobel Laureates, especially the Dalai Lama, and has written several illuminating books including a history of light called *Catching the Light*. Visit arthurzajonc.org.

p. 105: **"The word *art* . . ."** I first explored this in my book *Drinking from the River of Light*. Louisville, CO: Sounds True, 2019, p. 116.

p. 106: **"our *enthusiasm* . . ."** This description first appeared in my daybook *The Book of Awakening*. Newburyport, MA: Red Wheel, 2000.

p. 109: **"The French poet Paul Valéry . . ."** This passage first appeared as part of the chapter "Below All Names" in my book *Surviving Storms: Finding the Strength to Meet Adversity*. New York: St. Martin's Essentials, 2022, pp. 176–178.

p. 111: **"see a world in a grain of sand"** William Blake, from "Auguries of Innocence" in *William Blake: The Complete Illuminated Books*, edited by David Bindman. London: Thames & Hudson, 2001.

p. 113: **"Japanese word *ma* . . ."** For an in-depth exploration of *ma*, please see Beth Kempton's forthcoming, beautifully written book *MA: Japanese Wisdom for a Spacious Life* (London: Piatkus Books, 2027). Beth is a lifelong student of Japanese thought and literature in the many ways it serves as a threshold to the beauty of being that makes life bearable. She is an impeccable guide to the spaces in between and the eternal resources that wait there for us.

p. 116: **"The seat of contemplation . . ."** I first explored these notions in the chapter "The Eyes of the Deep" in my book *The Exquisite Risk*. New York: Harmony Books, 2005, p. 186.

## The Nature of Relationship

p. 124: **"Things may be named . . ."** Lao Tzu, from chapter 1, *Laws Divine and Human (Tao teh Ching)*, translated by Xu Yuanchong. Beijing: China Intercontinental Press, 2019, p. 2.

p. 134: **"We have no right . . ."** The story of the pharmacist and the chemist and their quote are from Maria Popova's column, The Marginalian, themarginalian.org/2021/10/26/why-leaves-change-color/.

p. 135: **"You will experience moments . . ."** The physicist Arthur Zajonc reports that "The history of this citation is complex. We have it from the private notes of a Waldorf teacher who in turn got it from a colleague of Steiner's who received it from him. It is usually taken as truly being from Steiner, though we do not have it in his handwriting directly." First cited in the chapter "An Exercise in Faithfulness" in my book *More Together Than Alone*. New York: Atria, 2018.

p. 140: **"In his *Analects* . . ."** These concepts are clearly stated in the *Encyclopædia Britannica Online* (Encyclopædia Britannica Inc., 2012), britannica.com/topic/ren.

p. 141: **"Ren means . . ."** Mencius, from "Confucian Key Terms: Ren," Kurtis Hagen, 2007.

p. 141: **"Ren signifies . . ."** This insight and other details about ren are from Tu Wei-ming, the director of the Harvard-Yenching Institute, an independent institute jointly founded by Harvard

University and Yenching University in 1928 for the higher education of humanity and social science of East Asia and Southeast Asia. He is the author of several books including *Humanity and Self-Cultivation: Essays in Confucian Thought*; *The Living Tree: The Changing Meaning of Being Chinese Today*; and *Confucian Thought: Selfhood as Creative Transformation*.

p. 143: **"the word *tarenga* . . ."** From Chef Pierre Thiam in his new book on modern Senegalese cuisine, *Senegal*. See "Splendid Table," NPR, August 28, 2015, splendidtable.org/episode/589.

### Commitments to Living

p. 151: **"This is the story of Sejong . . ."** This story of Sejong (1397–1450) first appeared in the chapter "Removing the Oldest Wall" in my book *More Together Than Alone*. New York: Atria, 2018, pp. 210–212.

p. 152: **"undertook for Sejong . . ."** Sejong also supported Jang Yeong-sil, a gifted inventor from the lower class. Despite court opposition, Sejong funded the inventor's work in creating water clocks and sundials, and the world's first rain gauge.

p. 152: **"Hangul . . ."** From the chart "Reform Movements" in *Lapham's Quarterly: Means of Communication*, volume V, number 2: spring 2012, p. 40. Details on the life of Sejong the Great are from Wikipedia. See en.wikipedia.org/wiki/Sejong_the_Great.

p. 152: **"In his introduction to Hangul, Sejong wrote . . ."** "Because the speech of this country is different from that of China, [the spoken language] does not match the letters. Therefore, even if the ignorant want to communicate, many of them . . . cannot state their concerns. Saddened by this, I have [had] 28 letters newly made. It is my wish that all the people may easily learn these letters and that [they] be convenient for daily use." From the introduction to *Hunminjeongeum* by King Sejong the Great, offering Hangul as the new Korean language, October 9, 1446. See en.wikipedia.org/wiki/Hunmin_Jeongeum.

p. 153: **"an acequia . . . *ahimsa*"** I first explored the origin and metaphor of an acequia (p. 183) and the notion of ahimsa (pp. 39, 246) in my book *More Together Than Alone*. New York: Atria, 2018.

p. 153: **"All suffering recoils . . ."** Tiruvalluvar, in "The Hindu Ethic of Non-Violence," Subramuniyaswami, H. H. Gurudeva Sivaya. In *Hinduism Today*, Public Service Department, himalayanacademy.com/resources/pamphlets/AhimsaNonViolence.html.

p. 156: **"As a child, I received a library card . . ."** This excerpt first appeared as part of the chapter "Keeper of the Tablets" in my book *Surviving Storms: Finding the Strength to Meet Adversity*. New York: St. Martin's Essentials, 2022, p. 237.

p. 162: **"Libraries and those who preserve knowledge . . ."** Historical details in this chapter are drawn from a remarkably thorough history of libraries found at Wikipedia. See en.wikipedia.org/wiki/History_of_libraries.

p. 166: **"the Japanese word *ikigai* . . ."** I am grateful to Jennifer Cory for introducing me to the Japanese tradition of ikigai and a wealth of history about how it is understood in the East and the West and the word's origins.

p. 167: **"where our gifts can be of use . . ."** For an in-depth exploration of this theme, please see the last section, "Being Kind and of Useful," of my book *The One Life We're Given*. New York: Atria, 2016.

p. 167: **"four overlapping circles . . ."** Marc Winn's diagram of ikigai appears in *Ikigai: The Japanese Secret to a Long and Happy Life* by Francesc Miralles and Hector Garcia. New York: Penguin, 2016.

p. 168: **"Yet, if we look more closely . . ."** Please see Michael Metcalf's insightful blog "Ikigai Meaning: 5 Steps to Unlocking Your Life's Joy," getmarlee.com/blog/what-is-ikigai.

p. 171: **"This ever-present choice . . ."** This description of Jacob wrestling with the unnamed angel appeared in the chapter "Wrestling with God" in my book *Finding Inner Courage*. Newburyport, MA: Red Wheel, 2010, pp. 21–22.

p. 173: **"In the Russian language . . ."** This quote and references to prehistoric, indigenous, and Icelandic languages are from the fascinating interview with the linguist Justin E. H. Smith, "Speaking of Tongues," by Finn Cohen, in *The Sun*, Chapel Hill, NC, Issue 569, May 2023, pp. 4–13.

p. 174: **"my book *Finding Inner Courage* . . ."** These two paragraphs originally appeared in the chapter "We Relate More Than We Author" in my book *Drinking from the River of Light*. Louisville, CO: Sounds True, 2019, pp. 56–57.

p. 178: **"the center cannot hold."** This line is from the famous poem "The Second Coming" by William Butler Yeats, written in 1919 in the aftermath of World War I and at the beginning of the Irish War of Independence.

p. 178: **"In the Sufi tradition, *muhasiba* . . ."** from "Sufi Practice and Contemporary Psychoanalysis" by Michele Rousseau, in *Sufi, A Journal of Sufism.* London: Khaniquahi Minatullahi Publications, Issue 88, Winter 2015, p. 42.

p. 179: **"In Spanish, *querencia* . . ."** from *Writing Toward Home*, Georgia Heard. Portsmouth, NH: Heinemann, 1995.

p. 183: **"It's worthy to note . . ."** These two paragraphs originally appeared in the chapter "The Paradox of Limitation" in my book *Surviving Storms: Finding the Strength to Meet Adversity*. New York: St. Martin's Essentials, 2022, p. 154.

p. 184: **"'Rhapsody in Blue'"** Here is a remarkable version of Gershwin playing "Rhapsody in Blue" himself on piano: youtube.com/watch?v=_kIpr6nSvjI.

p. 184: **"the Buddhist word for faith, *saddha* . . ."** I am indebted to the great Buddhist teacher Tara Brach for unpacking the deeper meaning of this.

p. 186: **"a huge crowd assembled . . ."** The story of Chenevix Trench and the meeting in the London Library is from a brilliant lecture by the journalist and author Simon Winchester based on his book *The Meaning of Everything: The Story of the Oxford English Dictionary*, broadcast on the TVO program *Big Ideas*, March 25, 2007. See tvo.org/bigideas.

p. 186: **"that eventually created the *Oxford English Dictionary* . . ."** The first complete edition of the *OED* was finally published on April 19, 1928.

p. 187: **"The Indian Revolt of 1857 . . ."** I also refer to this event in my spiritual novel in progress, *This Strange and Blessed Humanness*, p. 274.

p. 187: **"hanging thousands for sympathizing with the revolt . . ."** The research in India of Dr. K. M. Ashraf ("Ghalib & The Revolt of 1857," in *Rebellion 1857*. Ed. P. C. Joshi. New Delhi: People's Publishing House, 1957) proves that at least 27,000 people were hanged during the summer of 1857 for participating in or sympathizing with the revolt. Living in Delhi at the time, the famous Urdu poet Ghalib (1797–1869) witnessed it all; detailing the horror in his letters and in a diary he kept called *Dastambo*.

p. 189: **"sumu . . ."** from Saigyo, *Poems of a Mountain Home*, trans. Burton Watson. New York: Columbia University Press, 1991, p. 51.

p. 191: **"I suddenly knew . . ."** From *Such Stuff as Dreams Are Made On: The Autobiography and Journals of Helen M. Luke*. New York: Harmony, 2001, p. 3.

### Correcting the Missteps That Keep Us from Living

p. 197: **"In the beginning, everyone spoke the same language . . ."** This retelling of the Tower of Babel first appeared in the chapter "Putting Down the Brick" in my book *More Together Than Alone*. New York: Atria, 2018, pp. 204–205.

p. 200: **"As early as 1844, Karl Marx . . ."** Comparative Religion professor Tim Light of Western Michigan University notes that, in our haste to exile all Marxist thought, we've dropped some very important insights he had into the nature of society. My further discussion of Marx and his notion of alienation comes from my book *More Together Than Alone*. New York: Atria, 2018, p. 213.

p. 200: **"Marx thought of therapists as *alienists* . . ."** Alienation is a theme that runs throughout the work of Karl Marx (1818–1883), beginning with his *Economic and Philosophical Manuscripts* of 1844.

p. 201: **"For these estrangements . . ."** Many sociologists of the late nineteenth and early twentieth century were concerned about the alienating effects of modernization pointed to by Marx. German sociologists Georg Simmel (1858–1918) and Ferdinand Tönnies (1855–1936) wrote seminal works on individualization and urbanization. Simmel's *Philosophy of Money (Philosophie des Geldes)* explores how relationships become more and more diluted through money, while Tönnies's *Community and Society (Gemeinschaft und Gesellschaft)* describes the loss of primary relationships such as family bonds in favor of goal-oriented relationships.

p. 205: **"Psychotherapist Edward Tick . . ."** Ed and I have known each other for forty years. Through his devotion to the healing of veterans, he is adding to our understanding of what violence does to the soul and to the society that ignores these psycho-spiritual physics. Please see *War and the Soul: Healing Our Nation's Veterans from Post-Traumatic Stress Disorder* (Newburyport, MA: Quest Books, 2005); *The Practice of Dream Healing: Bringing Ancient Greek Mysteries into Modern Medicine* (Newburyport, MA: Quest Books, 2001); and *Sacred Mountain: Encounters with the Viet Nam Beast* (Santa Fe, NM: Moon Bear Press, 1989).

p. 210: **"embarazar"** The most common definition of embarazar is "to get pregnant."

p. 223: **"In Buddhism, *upekkhā* . . ."** American Buddhist monk Bhikkhu Bodhi, from *Toward a Threshold of Understanding*, cited on accesstoinsight.org, ©1998–2010.

## Meeting Difficulty and Change

p. 226: **"No one knows . . ."** Henk Brandt, from the poem "Purely Herself" in *Songs for Sophia* (2013). By permission of the author.

p. 227: **"Beyond his life . . ."** Details about the extent of Sequoyah's influence are from the article "How Sequoyah, who did not read or write, created a written language for the Cherokee Nation from scratch" from the PBS show *American Masters*, pbs.org/wnet /americanmasters/blog/how-sequoyah-who-did-not-read-or -write-created-a-written-language-for-the-cherokee-nation-from -scratch/.

p. 228: **"todatsu . . ."** Dogen, from *Moon in a Dewdrop: Writings of Zen Master Dogen,* edited by Kazuaki Tanahashi. San Francisco: North Point Press, 1985, p. 19.

p. 228: **"In his early work in Mexico . . ."** In a conversation with John Paul about concepts that don't quite translate into English, March 22, 2006. Please see *The Moral Imagination* and *The Journey Toward Reconciliation*, both by John Paul Lederach.

p. 232: **"Their story . . ."** Details about Sir James Murray and William Chester Minor are from the article "The True Story Behind the Professor and the Madman" by Morgan Awyong, edsays.catchplay .com/sg/article-3054-tdrg5vaa.

p. 239: **"creating the first modern mystery . . ."** Details about the history of the modern mystery come from "A Brief History of Mystery Books" by Amy Manikowski, biblio.com/blog/2020/01/a-brief -history-of-mystery-books.

p. 246: **"a form of everyday togetherness . . ."** From "Interweavings: A cultural phenomenology of everyday consumption and social atmosphere within Danish middleclass," Jeppe Trolle. Odensk: University Press of Southern Denmark, 2010.

## The Work and Practice of Being Alive

p. 268: **"The Lebanese greeting** *ya ayuni!*" I'm indebted to my friend, the wonderful poet Naomi Shihab Nye for introducing me to this joyous custom.

p. 273: **"The first word, 'Ah' . . ."** Kukai, from *The Enlightened Heart*, edited by Stephen Mitchell. New York: Harper & Row, 1989, pp. 36, 159. Kukai (774–835), also known as Kobo Daishi, was one of the first Japanese abbots and scholars to believe that we are all innately enlightened and that, regardless of status or education, we all have the capacity to awaken to that blossom we carry from birth.

# Permissions

Thorough efforts have been made to secure all permissions. Any omissions or corrections will be made in future editions.

Thanks for permission to excerpt the following from other previously published works:

Excerpts from my books *Falling Down and Getting Up* (2023), *Surviving Storms* (2022), and *The Book of Soul* (2020) are by permission of St. Martin's Essentials.

Excerpts from my book *Drinking from the River of Light* © 2019 Mark Nepo, excerpted with permission of the publisher, Sounds True Inc.

Excerpts from my book *The Book of Awakening* © 2020, 2011, 2000 by Mark Nepo is used with permission from Red Wheel Weiser, LLC, Newburyport, MA.

Excerpts from my book *Finding Inner Courage* © 2007, 2020 by Mark Nepo, used with permission from Red Wheel Weiser, LLC, Newburyport, MA.

Excerpts from my books *Seven Thousand Ways to Listen* (2012), *The Endless Practice,* (2014), *The One Life We're Given* (2016), and *More Together Than Alone* (2018) are by permission of Atria Books, an imprint of Simon & Schuster.

Excerpts from my book *The Exquisite Risk* (2005) are by permission of Harmony Books.

Excerpts from my book *Unlearning Back to God* (2006) are by permission of Sufi Publications.

Excerpt from the poem "Purely Herself" in *Songs for Sophia* (2013) by Henk Brandt. By permission of the author.

# About the Author

Brian Bankston

With over a million copies sold, Mark Nepo has moved and inspired readers and seekers all over the world with his #1 *New York Times* bestseller *The Book of Awakening*. Beloved as a poet, teacher, and storyteller, Mark has been called "one of the finest spiritual guides of our time," "a consummate storyteller," and "an eloquent spiritual teacher." His work is widely accessible and used by many, and his books have been translated into more than twenty languages.

A bestselling author, he has published twenty-eight books and recorded nineteen audio projects. He has received Life Achievement Awards from AgeNation (2015) and OMTimes (2023). In 2016, he was named by *Watkins: Mind Body Spirit* as one of the 100 Most Spiritually Influential Living People, and was also chosen as one of OWN's SuperSoul 100, a group of inspired leaders using their gifts and voices to elevate humanity. And from 2017 to 2023 Mark was a regular columnist for *Spirituality & Health Magazine.*

A five-time Nautilus Book Award winner, his recent works include *The Fifth Season: Creativity in the Second Half of Life*, cited by *Spirituality & Practice* as one of the Best Spiritual Books of 2025; *You Don't Have to Do It Alone*, cited by *Spirituality & Practice* as one of the Best Spiritual Books of 2024; *Falling Down and Getting Up*; *The Half-Life of Angels*, a Nautilus Book Award winner; *Surviving Storms*; *The Book of Soul*, a Nautilus Book Award winner; *Drinking from the River of Light*, a Nautilus Book Award winner; *More Together Than Alone*, cited by *Spirituality & Practice* as one of the Best Spiritual Books of 2018; *Things That Join the Sea and the Sky*, a Nautilus Book Award winner; *The Way Under the Way: The Place of True Meeting*, a Nautilus Book Award winner; *The One Life We're Given*, cited by *Spirituality & Practice* as one of the Best Spiritual Books of 2016; *Inside the Miracle*, selected by *Spirituality & Health Magazine* as one of the top ten Best Books of 2015; *The Endless Practice*, cited by *Spirituality & Practice* as one of the Best Spiritual Books of 2014; and *Seven Thousand Ways to Listen*, which won the 2012 Books for a Better Life Award.

Mark was part of Oprah Winfrey's The Life You Want tour in 2014 and has appeared several times with Oprah on her *Super Soul Sunday* program on OWN TV. He has also been interviewed by Robin Roberts on *Good Morning America. The Exquisite Risk* was listed by *Spirituality & Practice* as one of the Best Spiritual Books of 2005, calling it "one of the best books we've ever read on what it takes to live an authentic life." Mark devotes his writing and teaching to the journey of inner transformation and the life of relationship. He continues to offer readings, lectures, and retreats.

PLEASE VISIT MARK AT:

MarkNepo.com

live.marknepo.com

harrywalker.com/speakers/mark-nepo